America's Founding Fathers

GEORGE WASHINGTON

Creating a Nation

Wim Coleman and Pat Perrin

Enslow Publishers, Inc.

40 Industrial Road   PO Box 38
Box 398   Aldershot
Berkeley Heights, NJ 07922   Hants GU12 6BP
USA   UK

http://www.enslow.com

Library of Congress Cataloging-in-Publication Data

Coleman, Wim.
   George Washington: Creating a Nation / Wim Coleman & Pat Perrin.
      v. cm.— (America's founding fathers)
   Includes bibliographical references and index.
   Contents: Conspiracy—From country boy to Virginia gentleman—
Growing up fast—The young officer—A man of power—The general
and the American Revolution—From chaos to a Constitution—The first
president—A hero's final years—Remembering Washington.
      ISBN 0-7660-2290-0
      1. Washington, George, 1732-1799—Juvenile literature.
   2. Presidents—United States—Biography—Juvenile literature.
   3. Generals—United States—Biography—Juvenile literature.
   [1. Washington, George, 1732–1799. 2. Presidents.] I. Perrin, Pat.
   II. Title. III. Series.
   E312.66.C59 2004
   973.4'1'092—dc22

                                        2003011810

Printed in the United States of America

10 9 8 7 6 5 4 3 2 1

To Our Readers: We have done our best to make sure all Internet addresses
in this book were active and appropriate when we went to press. However, the
author and the publisher have no control over and assume no liability for
the material available on those Internet sites or on other Web sites they may
link to. Any comments or suggestions can be sent by e-mail to
comments@enslow.com or to the address on the back cover.

*C*ontents

From April 1782 to August 1783, General George Washington's headquarters was located at Newburgh, New York.

Conspiracy

NEAR THE END OF the Revolutionary War, a secret plot threatened America. If it succeeded, the new republic would be destroyed.

The year was 1783. The major Revolutionary War battles seemed to be over, although smaller skirmishes continued in a few places. Peace talks were dragging on in faraway Paris, France. British troops in America still outnumbered American forces. The British still occupied the important seaport of New York City and several western forts.

So the British threat to America still remained, and war might begin again. But a new threat rose from *within* America. It was a conspiracy against the government.

The Revolutionary War

During the 1770s, Great Britain's colonies in America became unhappy with British taxes, laws, and other policies. In 1775, the colonies raised troops—called the Continental army—to fight for their rights as British citizens. In 1776, the colonies decided to separate from Great Britain. They passed the Declaration of Independence, stating their determination to form a new country. After that, the Continental army continued fighting for America's freedom in the Revolutionary War.

Most of the fighting stopped in 1781, after British general Charles Cornwallis surrendered at Yorktown, Virginia. In 1782, Congress appointed Benjamin Franklin, John Adams, and John Jay as

Something to Worry About

General George Washington had been in command of the Continental Army since 1775. He had trained his troops under terrible conditions. He led them to victories against overwhelming forces. Even after most of the fighting ended, Washington and his army had to stay on guard until the British left.

As months went by, the American troops grew bored, restless, and worried. George Washington wrote, "The Army, as usual, are without Pay; and a great part of the Soldiery without Shirts; and tho' the patience of them is equally thread bear, the States seem perfectly indifferent to their cries."[1]

peace commissioners. They went to Paris, France, to work out the terms of a peace treaty with diplomats from England. The peace committee was making real progress, but nobody in the United States had any way of knowing that. None of today's electronic, worldwide communication systems existed then. Even the telegraph had not yet been invented. Ships powered by wind and sail were a slow way to send messages.

In October 1781, General Cornwallis surrendered at Yorktown.

The men had been promised pensions or bonuses at the end of the war. But for months, the soldiers had not even received their regular pay. They were afraid that when peace came, they would be discharged and sent home with nothing.

The soldiers were right to worry. Congress had no money and no way of raising it.

The Conspirators

After the Battle of Yorktown, many army officers and soldiers were at General George Washington's headquarters, a military camp at Newburgh, New York. In early March 1783, some officers decided that it was time for action. Ignoring General

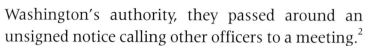

Washington's authority, they passed around an unsigned notice calling other officers to a meeting.[2]

Then, in another anonymous letter, the conspirators described two possibilities. If the peace treaty was not signed and the war continued, the army should disband. Its members should set up their own country in the western wilderness. That would leave the United States defenseless. If peace did come, the army should refuse to disband. They should keep together and stay armed until Congress gave them everything they wanted. That choice might easily lead to a military dictatorship in the United States.

When he learned of the letters, Washington was horrified.[3] He sympathized with the army, but he would take no part in threatening his country. Washington knew that these officers had enough intelligence, training, and discipline to overthrow Congress and take over state governments. Washington had made many personal sacrifices to achieve an American victory. And now would it all be lost, not to the British, but to America's own military?

General Washington was fifty-one years old, and he hoped to retire soon from public life. But first, he had to prevent a disaster.

Spectacles Save the Day

Washington called the officers to a meeting of his own, set for noon on March 15, 1783. He said that General Horatio Gates would be in charge of the meeting. Washington was well aware that Gates was one of those who favored the conspirators' point of view. Washington also knew that putting Gates in charge would encourage the whole group of conspirators to attend.

Early in his career, General Washington had decided that a military commander must be a strong leader. But at this meeting, Washington could give no orders. Rather than telling those below him in the chain of command what to do, he had to try to change their minds.[4] It was not a job he looked forward to.[5]

The officers assembled in a large wooden building that had been finished only a few weeks before. It smelled of fresh-cut wood. Roaring fires in several fireplaces kept the room quite warm. The officers crowded the space, talking, or just waiting for the meeting to begin.[6]

At Newburgh in 1783, General Horatio Gates favored the Continental army's conspirators.

It is well known that George Washington did not like to make public addresses. Even so, he strode into the room at noon and stepped up to the small stage and podium at one end. The room fell silent. Washington began to read from his notes. His voice was low, and the men had to strain to hear.[7] Washington reminded his men that he had never left their side, except when Congress had called him away on other business. He said that his own military reputation was forever connected with theirs. He also complimented the army. He assumed that they must feel horror for whoever was trying "to overturn the liberties of our Country . . . and deluge our rising Empire in Blood."[8] He urged them not to let anyone spoil the glory they had already earned.

Washington finished speaking and looked out over the silent room. It had not worked.

He could tell from the officers' faces that he had not changed their minds.[9] What else could he do? Washington remembered a letter that he had in his pocket.

Fumbling in his coat pocket, he pulled out the letter. He unfolded the paper slowly and started to read, but he seemed to be having trouble seeing the words.

Washington stopped and reached into his pocket again. This time, he pulled out a pair of glasses and put them on. Most of the officers had never seen Washington wear spectacles before, though he often used them for reading. The general began the letter again, and then he stopped and peered over the spectacles at his audience.

Still speaking softly, Washington said, "Gentlemen, you must pardon me. I have grown gray in your service and now find myself growing blind."[10]

Tears ran down many of the battle-hardened faces in that hall.[11] The words Washington read were not important. It was the humanity of their commander that touched the hearts of men who had been about to mutiny.

Washington finished the letter, slowly removed his glasses, tucked them away, and walked out of the room without another word. That night, the officers made a formal statement of loyalty to Congress. The immediate crisis was over.

Survival by Compromise

Even while Washington was speaking to the troops, Virginia congressman James Madison was busily working with other members of Congress on a plan to raise money. In the end, Washington's strong leadership had convinced the officers to compromise. At first, they were given leaves of absence instead of discharges, so they received no payment right away. Later, they were paid at least part of the money that they had expected.[12] When they retired, the officers received five years of full pay instead of the half-pay for life that Congress had originally promised.[13]

The ideals of the Revolutionary War were upheld, and the new republic survived its first threat from within.

From Country Boy to Virginia Gentleman

THESE DAYS, FEW PEOPLE think of George Washington as an inexperienced country boy—but that is exactly how he started out. On February 22, 1732, George was born in the colony of Virginia. That made him a citizen of Great Britain.

As a young boy, George Washington lived in the country. He first saw a town when he was about seven years old.[1] Although some of his male relatives had been well educated in England, George was not to have that advantage. He went to a local school for a few years and had private tutors. Although he did not attend college, he did not stop learning whatever he needed to know.

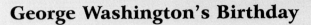
George Washington's Birthday

According to the Julian (or Old Style) calendar used at that time, George Washington was born on February 11, 1731. In 1752, Britain and its colonies adopted the Gregorian (or New Style) calendar, adding eleven days to that particular year. Along with that change, the new year began on January 1 instead of March 25. As a result, George's birthday moved from February 11, 1731, to February 22, 1732.[2]

Washington Family Matters

The first Washington in the colonies came to Virginia from England in 1657. Over the following generations, none of the Washingtons became very wealthy, but they were successful middle-class property owners. The Washington men often served in public offices, such as justice of the peace, sheriff, and member of the House of Burgesses (the lower house of Virginia's legislative body).[3]

George's father, Augustine Washington, was a tall, strong, kindhearted man. He was a justice of the peace, a plantation owner, and a partner in a group that mined iron ore and manufactured iron products.[4] Whenever he could afford to, Augustine Washington added land to the family property. He married twice and fathered nine children. Two boys from his first marriage lived to adulthood. After his first wife died, Augustine married Mary

In the 1700s, much of North America was owned by England and by France.

Ball. They had five children. The first was a boy, and they named him George.

During George's earliest years, his family lived on farms far from any town. In 1738, his family moved to Ferry Farm on the Rappahannock River. The town of Fredericksburg was just across the river, and George went to school there for two or three years.[5] Then, in 1743, George's father suddenly fell ill and died. George was eleven.

Augustine Washington is mentioned only a few times in George Washington's letters and journals. There is no sign that they were very close, but also no sign that their relationship was troubled.[6] George remembered his father as a tall, fair, well-built man who loved children.[7]

In his will, Augustine Washington left Ferry Farm, some additional land, and ten slaves to George. Mary Ball Washington, George's mother, was put in charge of everything until George turned twenty-one. George's mother was stern and could be very demanding. A childhood friend of George's said, "Of the mother, I was ten times more afraid than of my own parents."[8]

After her husband's early death, Mary Washington could not afford to send George to England for an education. In spite of that, George received a good basic education. He discovered that he had a talent for math. He also set goals for himself, such as learning to write quickly and smoothly.

At that time, many schoolchildren practiced writing by copying parts of books. George copied all 110 of the "Rules of Civility and Decent Behavior in Company and in Conversation." That was not just to practice his handwriting, but also to learn proper etiquette. He lived by many of those rules for the rest of his life. They included such advice as "Think before you Speak . . ." and "Every Action done in Company, ought to be with Some Sign of Respect, to those that are Present."[9]

Slavery in America

A slave is a person who is owned by another person. Early in human history, slaves were mostly prisoners taken in battle. After the Americas were settled, the colonists felt they needed more and more labor to work the land. The colonists had first tried enslaving American Indians, but the American Indians could easily escape and return to their homes. The capture and sale of Africans as slaves then became a big business. Men, women, and children were bought and sold on a large scale by George Washington's time.

Most slaves in the British colonies were brought from Africa. The first Africans were brought to Virginia in 1619. At first, they were treated like indentured servants (workers under contract) who could earn their freedom, but within a year or two, Africans were being imported as slaves. After 1700, the number of imported slaves began to rise—and they were to be slaves for life. By the middle of the 1700s, slaves made up about 40 percent of the Virginia population. As a child, George Washington was familiar with the practice of slavery. Later in life, he struggled with moral questions about slavery and decided that it was terribly wrong.

At the same time, George discovered that he needed to know about other kinds of things, as well.

Becoming a Young Gentleman

George's half-brother, Lawrence, was fourteen years older than George. Lawrence Washington had been educated in England, where he had learned how to behave like a proper English gentleman. Lawrence had even been a captain in Great Britain's colonial army during a war with Spain. George visited his brother's home every chance he got.

Lawrence Washington, like George, had inherited a lot of property from his father. He built a new home, which he called Mount Vernon. He married Anne Fairfax—a member of a very wealthy and powerful Virginia family.

Anne's father was Colonel William Fairfax, who managed over 5 million acres in Virginia for his cousin, Lord Thomas Fairfax. The land had been granted to Lord Fairfax by the British crown. The magnificent Fairfax manor home, Belvoir, was not far from Mount Vernon. When George went to visit his sister-in-law's family, Lord Fairfax was often there. Lord Fairfax took an immediate liking to the Virginia youth.

Life at Belvoir was a new world for George. His home at Ferry Farm had been reasonably comfortable, but nothing like this. The difference was not just in the sizes of the houses and the fanciness of the furniture. It was in the way people dressed and behaved and in the things they talked about.

Like other students of his time, George Washington copied pages from books to practice his handwriting. This page is from the "Rules of Civility and Decent Behavior in Company and in Conversation."

Conversations at Mount Vernon and Belvoir went far beyond farming. The older men recalled the glories of military life. They discussed frontier territory in Virginia's Shenandoah Valley and farther west. They hoped for new treaties with American Indian nations, which would allow the British to expand beyond the Allegheny Mountains. And they talked about ideas in books and newspapers that they had read.[10]

George had not inherited great wealth, so he decided to better himself as much as he could. He set about learning how a young gentleman should behave. At age fifteen, he took dancing lessons.[11] He learned to fence. He read what the gentlemen around him were reading.[12] He watched quietly and listened carefully before he said anything. That habit lasted the rest of George Washington's life.[13]

During this time, George's family debated the question of his future profession. Joining the British navy was one option, but his mother disapproved of this choice. George had to learn another skill. He already had taught himself to use his father's surveying instruments, and surveyed parts of his relatives' farms. He mastered all the mathematics needed to make complicated measurements and draw accurate maps of property. When George was about fifteen, he even got paid for a small surveying job.[14]

In the colonies, surveying was considered a suitable profession for a gentleman. Everyone who owned property needed the help of a skillful, honest, and dependable surveyor. When the king of England granted colonial land to people such as Lord Fairfax, the location was rather vague. For example, it might be described as all the land between certain rivers or mountains. The landowner was expected to mark the boundaries and find out exactly how much land was included.[15]

In addition to locating and measuring property, a surveyor could learn where the best land was. He could find out where land could be bought or rented. A surveyor could also buy land for himself or take land in payment for his work. Surveying was a way to become a major landowner.

In 1748, Lord Fairfax was visiting Belvoir. He wanted to divide some of his property in the Shenandoah Valley into small farms that he could rent to tenants. Colonel Fairfax decided to send an experienced surveyor, James Genn, to measure off the land for farms. Two years earlier, Genn had marked the boundaries of the Fairfax property. He knew the country well.

Colonel Fairfax also decided to send his cousin William's son, George William Fairfax, and George Washington to work with Genn. George William Fairfax was seven years older than George Washington, and George was delighted at the chance to travel with the young gentleman.[16]

George was sixteen. He was tall, strong, athletic, and an excellent horseman. He could ride for hours at a time, but he was used to returning to a comfortable bed at night. He had visited cousins

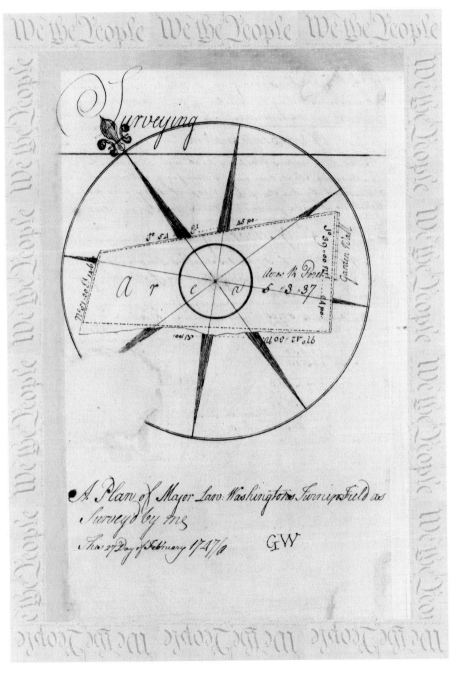

George Washington practiced surveying on his relatives' farms, including his brother Lawrence's turnip patch. George was fifteen years old when he made this drawing.

Surveying was considered a suitable profession for a gentleman during George Washington's youth.

for weeks at a time, but this was his first trip away from his family. It turned out to be more difficult than he had expected.

George Washington's First Frontier Adventure

On March 11, 1748, George Washington and George William Fairfax set out together. They rode past familiar homes and landmarks into more sparsely settled areas of Virginia. Soon, they were passing fewer and smaller farms. They traveled forty miles that day and stopped at an inn that was popular with travelers.

The next morning, James Genn joined them at the inn. The three rode northwest over the Blue Ridge Mountains. On the other side of the mountains, the group explored Fairfax lands near the Shenandoah River and the town of Winchester. It

Tuesday 15th. . . . we got our Suppers & was Lighted in to a Room & I not being so good a Woodsman as the rest of my Company striped my self very orderly & went in to the Bed as they call'd it when to my Surprize I found it to be nothing but a Little Straw—Matted together without Sheets or any thing else but only one Thread Bear blanket with double its Weight of Vermin such as Lice Fleas &c. I was glad to get up (as soon as the Light was carried from us) & put on my Cloths & Lay as my Companions. Had we not have been very tired, I am sure we should not have slep'd much that night. I made a Promise not to Sleep so from that time forward chusing rather to sleep in the open Air before a fire. . . .[17]

George Washington and the others surveyors spent their first night in the cottage of a local landowner. In this journal passage, George wrote that he did not find the experience comfortable.

was raining steadily. By the end of the first day's work, George was ready for bed immediately after supper.

The next day the group continued, riding in the rain along what George called "the Worst Road that ever was trod by Man or Beast."[18] On March 21, they reached the trading post of Thomas Cresap, near the Potomac River. The next day, the rain finally stopped. The clear sky was welcome after so many soggy days, but it did not mean that the surveyors could continue on their way. The river was too swift and high to cross. George and his friends had to stay right where they were.

George was getting bored and restless.[19] Then, as if from nowhere, company appeared. George wrote in his journal, "We were agreeably surpris'd at the sight of thirty odd Indians."[20] He had seen American Indians, but not so many at one time.[21] This group had been on a long, hard journey and had stopped by the trading post to visit their friend Cresap. That evening, the American Indians danced for the colonists.[22]

The American Indians cleared a huge circle and built a great fire in the center. They needed a drum, so they borrowed a pot from Cresap. They filled the pot halfway with water, then stretched a deerskin across the top. This was called a water drum, and the amount of water in the container controlled the sound.[23] One man brought out a dried gourd decorated with hair from a horse's tail. Metal shot inside the gourd made a fine rattle when it was shaken.

The American Indians were ready now. For them, this was probably an ordinary social event, which often included dancing, storytelling, singing, and speeches.[24] First, the American Indians sat around the edge of the circle while one of them spoke. George did not understand a word the man said, but he thought it must be a "grand Speech telling them in what Manner they are to Daunce after he has finish'd."[25]

Suddenly, a warrior jumped up and looked around, pretending that he had just been awakened from sleep. He ran into the ring and leaped about. Other American Indians followed, and the musicians started to pound the drum and shake the rattle. George watched in fascination as the American Indians danced.

James Genn, George William Fairfax, George Washington, and the American Indians all spent the next day at Cresap's. After that, the surveyors were able to cross the river by canoe. But it was not easy to make the horses swim through the strong current. Finally, they got safely across.

While the three surveyors were finishing up their work, they sometimes stayed with frontiersmen who lived in the area, and sometimes camped out. Their tent was blown down twice. By the time they headed home, George Washington had proved that he could measure a piece of property, even in the rain. He had also learned something about roughing it in the wilderness.

Growing
Up Fast

SOON AFTER HIS FIRST frontier adventure, George Washington got another chance to use his surveying skills. In 1748, some important Virginia families—including Philip and John Alexander, Hugh West, and the Fairfaxes—decided to build a new town on the Potomac River. They named it Alexandria. George Washington worked as an assistant surveyor, measuring out lots to be put up for sale.[1]

After that, Washington decided to make surveying his profession. He took a surveyor's examination at the College of William and Mary in Williamsburg, Virginia. Washington passed the test and got a certificate, making him a fully qualified surveyor. Soon Washington would return to the frontier with a surveying party, but this time he would be in charge.

Working on the Wild Frontier

In 1749, at seventeen, George Washington was appointed the official surveyor for the newly created Virginia county of Culpeper. It was his first public office, and he was very young for such an important position. The influence of the powerful Fairfax family probably helped him get the job.[2]

Washington surveyed property in Culpeper County and beyond, in the Fairfax lands known as the Northern Neck of Virginia. This property lay between the Potomac and the Rappahannock rivers. It extended from the headwaters (streams that run into a river) of the Potomac and the Rappahannock to the Chesapeake Bay.

Washington explored the wilderness for weeks at a time, rarely changing into clean clothes. He camped out or stayed in the cabins of backcountry settlers, seldom sleeping in a bed. He shared meals with wandering bands of American Indians. And he had the responsibility of supervising a group of workmen, all older than he was.[3] George Washington still found the traveling strenuous, and he thought frontier settlers were rough-mannered and uncivilized. But he was making good money.[4] Washington's time was divided between hard work in the wilderness and visits to his family. Sometimes, his family visits were pure fun. But a very sad situation was also developing at home.

Deadly Diseases and Terrible Loss

Washington's brother, Lawrence, had been in poor health for several years. By spring 1749, Lawrence was suffering from tuberculosis, a lung disease that was usually fatal at this time. He traveled to London to see doctors there. When Lawrence returned to Virginia, his health had not improved.

In the summer of 1750, Washington went with Lawrence to Warm Springs, Virginia. They hoped that the natural mineral waters would improve Lawrence's health. When that did not help, the family became afraid that Lawrence would not survive another winter in Virginia.

Many people with lung diseases went to the island of Barbados, a British colony in the Caribbean Sea. Lawrence's wife had recently had a baby girl and could not travel. So Washington went to Barbados with his brother.[5] They arrived by ship in November and hurried to have Lawrence examined by a local physician.

Lawrence Washington, George's half brother, suffered from tuberculosis.

To their relief, the doctor believed that Lawrence's case was not too far along to be successfully treated.

Washington and Lawrence found lodging in a private home close to the water. In spite of his concern about his brother, George found the tropical island beautiful and exciting. From their rooms, the brothers could look out over ships moving in and out of the harbor. They were wined, dined, and entertained by many British members of the island society.[6]

Washington discovered that his lessons in self-improvement in Virginia had worked very well. Even among people he did not know, he could conduct himself properly in social gatherings. In Barbados, Washington saw his first play. He became fascinated with the theater and would go as often as he could in the years to come.[7]

One morning, George Washington felt oddly weak. He had a high fever. By evening his head felt as if it might split, and he had pains all over his body. A few days later, red spots appeared on his forehead. The spots rapidly grew into papules—small, solid, bumps.

Washington was sick for another week. Then, the fever dropped. Scabs began to fall off his swellings. Washington had survived, and he was now immune to smallpox. He would not have to worry about being exposed to it in the future, which was important during his military service.

As for Lawrence, he was no better. He was homesick for his wife and little girl, but he decided to go to the island of Bermuda to see if its climate would help. Washington went back to Virginia to help take care of business matters. When the weather was better in Virginia, Lawrence expected to return there and try the warm springs again.

Tuberculosis and Smallpox

Lawrence Washington had tuberculosis, which was then called consumption.[8] In its most common form, tuberculosis affects the lungs. Often, very few symptoms show up in the early stages of the infection. Some people's immune systems can fight off the disease. In some cases, it disappears permanently; in others, it breaks out again years later. If the infection progresses, it destroys the lungs and other organs, resulting in death. Now we have anti-tuberculosis drugs and vaccines, but no real treatment was available in Washington's time.

While in the islands, George Washington contracted smallpox, a very contagious disease that causes a high fever and pus-filled blisters on the skin.[9] The itchy, painful blisters crust over and eventually fall off, leaving scars. Throughout history, smallpox has caused more deaths than any other infectious disease. Many American Indians died from smallpox brought from Europe by colonists. Fortunately, those who have had smallpox are immune from future infection.

When Lawrence did return home, he was very ill. He hurriedly put his property in order and wrote his will. In July 1752, Lawrence died. Washington had the sad responsibility of arranging for the funeral and helping to organize Lawrence's property.

Lawrence's will provided for his wife, Anne, and daughter, Sarah. Washington gained control of Mount Vernon when Sarah died during childhood, and Anne remarried.

Responsibilities and Connections

While he worked as a surveyor, George Washington bought land with his own money. His first purchase, at age eighteen, had been nearly 1,500 acres on a tributary of the Shenandoah.[10] He continued to buy land, and sometimes he accepted land as payment for surveying. He was well on his way to becoming the gentleman landowner that he had dreamed of being. At the same time, Washington took on some of his deceased brother's former military responsibilities.

Lawrence had been adjutant of the Virginia Colony—the man in charge of the militia. A militia is a local defense force made up of volunteers who usually serve for short periods of time, protecting their home territory. The colony was growing fast, and the population was now too large for one adjutant to oversee. So Virginia was divided into four areas, with a separate militia for each area. Washington was made the adjutant of the southern district, between the James River and the North Carolina boundary.

The military rank of major came with the job.[11] One of Major Washington's jobs was to train the men in the militia. But first he had to learn what he should teach them. He studied every book he could find on military tactics.[12] That was the beginning of a military career that would not only affect George Washington's future, but the future of the colonies, as well.

The Young
Officer

AT AGE TWENTY-ONE, George Washington was six feet three and a half inches tall. At that time, adult men who had been born in the colonies averaged five feet seven inches in height, while European men averaged five feet four inches.[1] Washington was also physically powerful and athletic. Throughout his military career, many soldiers commented on what a remarkably good rider he was.

Washington had penetrating gray-blue eyes and auburn hair.[2] He was polite and acted as he had taught himself to behave—like an English gentleman. He had learned to control his temper and to keep his thoughts to himself unless he knew those around him very well. He was an impressive young man.

Deeper Into the Wilderness

In the mid-1700s, the Virginia colony covered much more territory than the state does now. In fact, two European nations had a major disagreement on the question of just how far west and north Virginia extended. Both France and England wanted the land on the western side of the Allegheny Mountains, along the Ohio River.

The French claimed the land because their agent, Sieur de La Salle (also known as René-Robert Cavelier), had explored the Ohio River area in the late 1680s. In 1753, the French were eager to own all the property along the Ohio and Mississippi rivers. That would connect their lands in Canada with their settlements in Louisiana.

The British colonies were all on the east coast of North America. If the French got the land they wanted, the British would be confined to the Atlantic coast, unable to expand westward. The British said that the Ohio River area was part of the Virginia colony. They based their claims on old treaties that they had made with the American Indians who lived there—members of the Iroquois League.

In 1753, Virginia governor Robert Dinwiddie heard that the French were moving down from Lake Erie toward the Ohio River, building forts along the way. King George II directed Dinwiddie to warn the French that they were on British land.

The Iroquois League

The Iroquois League was an association of American Indian nations, including the Mohawk, Oneida, Onondaga, Cayuga, Seneca, Tuscarora, and other groups. They lived in the area that became New York State and other nearby lands. Some of the Iroquois were hostile toward the French. During the French and Indian wars, they fought on the side of the British. During the American Revolution, most Iroquois again took the British side.

But who could Dinwiddie send as a royal messenger? It would have to be someone of social standing. But what suitable man could make the difficult trip through the wilderness to reach the French?

George Washington seemed to be a possible candidate. He had the manners of a gentleman and the appearance of someone born to command.[3] He also had some wilderness experience as a surveyor. The messenger to the French—if he survived the journey—would likely earn a high military rank. He might well become famous. Washington heard that he was under consideration and volunteered. Dinwiddie accepted him for the job.

Late in October 1753, Washington and his team of six other men started off to find the French commander. Christopher Gist was an experienced frontiersman who understood several American Indian languages. Another was a Dutchman who did not speak English very well, but could communicate in French. Some of the rest had been frontier traders.

Fame, Honor, and Character in the Eighteenth Century

In George Washington's mind, fame was connected with good character. In other words, he had to become famous for doing the right things. So fame and honor were closely connected. Washington always made a conscious effort to earn respect and approval, but only from those people *he* respected. For Washington, the idea of becoming famous by improper means would have been unthinkable.[4]

In the 1700s, character also meant the way a person chose to be seen in public. Washington decided on exactly the kind of person he wanted to be and was careful to behave "in character"—much like an actor in a play. That way, he believed, his public character would gradually overcome any less desirable personal traits. In other words, one could become one's best self by constantly behaving in an honorable manner.[5]

Sculptor Jean-Antoine Houdon's clay bust of George Washington

Washington's group had no major problems on the way to find the French. They even had a chance to talk with powerful members of the American Indian nations that lived in that area. Washington met a Seneca chief that the British called Half King. The chief was very interested in trade, but he was wary of foreigners taking over his people's lands. Half King sided with the British in the land dispute, mostly because he was convinced that the French had boiled and eaten his father.[6]

In December, Washington reached the French Fort Le Boeuf, near Lake Erie. He put on his formal Virginia major's dress uniform that he had brought all that way.[7] He gave the royal message to the French commander.

The French were sure that they had a right to the land in question, and they did not take the message seriously. The French commander told Washington that he rejected Governor Dinwiddie's royal message.[8] Meanwhile, Washington had taken a good look at the French defenses. He also saw that they had more than two hundred canoes, which would make it easy for them to float down the Ohio River when the ice melted.[9] It seemed obvious that the French would move southward in the spring. Even though the weather had turned bad for traveling, Washington was determined to leave immediately and get word back to Virginia.

Washington and his men started home, but their horses were tired, hungry, and overloaded. The animals staggered through deep snow. Washington and Gist decided to strike out on their own, on foot.[10] The other men could travel more slowly, bringing the horses and supplies.

When Washington and Gist reached an American Indian settlement, a guide offered to show them the shortest way. He even offered to carry Washington's gun for him. Suspicious, Washington refused to part with his weapon.[11] After a while, both Gist and Washington began to suspect that they were not headed in the right direction. Then, they came out of the trees into a bright clearing. It was hard to see in the sudden light. Their guide ran ahead, whirled, and fired his rifle at them.

"Are you shot?" Washington asked Gist.

"No," the startled Gist replied. [12]

Now the shooter was trying to reload his rifle. Washington and Gist charged forward and over-powered him. But what were they to do with him? Gist wanted to kill him on the spot. But Washington considered it wrong to kill a prisoner, so he insisted on freeing the treacherous guide. Then Washington and Gist had to get out of that area fast, before the guide could return with friends.

It was a hard trip home. When Washington and Gist reached a river that was too flooded to cross, they built a raft using their one small hatchet. As they were poling their way across the river, Washington slipped and fell into the icy water. With one long arm, Washington grabbed desper-ately for the raft. He managed to catch the edge, and Gist pulled him back on board. That night they camped on an island. The next morning, the river had frozen enough for them to cross on foot.[13]

Washington got back to Williamsburg in January 1754. He hurried to tell Governor Dinwiddie about the French and their canoes.

Washington's One and Only Surrender

In March, Governor Dinwiddie promoted George Washington to lieutenant colonel and made him second in command of the Virginia Regiment, which consisted of about three hundred men. Dinwiddie had already sent a group of thirty-three men to build a fort at the Forks of the Ohio (present-day Pittsburgh, Pennsylvania). Now Washington's job was to lead troops to protect those men and to escort wagons with supplies.

Governor Robert Dinwiddie (seated) made Washington (standing) second in command of the Virginia Regiment.

Washington quickly discovered that the 159 men assigned to him had neither military training nor proper equipment. Some did not even have shoes. Washington got together what equipment he could and gave them a little training in the short time available.

Before Washington reached the fort, he met

Dinwiddie's men on their way home. They said that more than a thousand French soldiers had overrun the entire area. The French had thrown out the Virginians and taken over their fort, naming it Fort Duquesne.

As Washington was hastily setting up defenses at a spot he called Fort Necessity, the American Indian chief Half King showed up. He told Washington that a French war party was nearby. With forty soldiers and a band of American Indians, Washington made a surprise attack on the small French force. It was not much of a battle, although Washington wrote to his brother John Augustine, "I heard the bullets whistle, and believe me, there is something charming in the sound."[14]

Some of the French were killed, including their leader, and others were taken prisoner. The French survivors claimed that Washington had attacked a peaceful party carrying a message to the Virginians. That small battle was the beginning of a much larger war.

Washington returned to Fort Necessity, which was soon attacked by superior French forces. It was pouring rain. Washington's trenches were filling with water. The weapons and powder were getting wet.

The French fought in the American Indian style, firing from well-hidden locations. Besides shooting at the men in the Virginia Regiment, the French killed their horses, cows, and even dogs. By evening, a third of Washington's men were dead or wounded. He had no way out and very little food left.

The French offered terms of surrender. They said that the survivors could return to Virginia. Washington accepted the terms, but it was the only time that he ever surrendered. When some American Indians learned about the French victory, they joined the French side of the conflict. The French were masters of the Ohio country—for a while.

Bravery Under Fire

When Washington returned to Williamsburg in July 1754, some colonists considered him a hero. Others thought that he had failed badly. Washington was offered another command, but at a lower military rank. Deeply dissatisfied, he resigned from the military and went home. Washington rented Mount Vernon from his sister-in-law and settled in to the life of a Virginia planter—for a very short time.

By the spring of 1755, the British government was ready to move against the French. The British had sent trained soldiers and officers from Great Britain. Commanding General Edward Braddock was impressed by Washington and persuaded him to accept a position as volunteer aide. Once again, Washington traveled into the Ohio wilderness.

When the men camped at night, Washington had a chance to study British military manuals. He learned that the British were trained to fight in an orderly military formation. Washington tried to warn

General Braddock that the Canadian French and the American Indians used a rougher, less conventional style, which he called bushfighting. This enemy was likely to fire from hidden places in the forest and then disappear among the trees. Braddock paid little attention to his aide.

As the British army marched nearer to Fort Duquesne in July 1755, loud war whooping startled them. They were shocked at being fired upon by an enemy they could not even see. Some soldiers panicked, threw away their weapons, and ran.[15] Washington later wrote his mother, "I luckily escap'd with't a wound, tho' I had four Bullets through my Coat, and two Horses shot under me."[16] General Braddock also lost several horses. Then, Braddock himself was hit.

Many other officers were wounded or killed. The soldiers were in total confusion. Determined to get his wounded general to safety, Washington put Braddock into a cart. He and several soldiers headed back to the British fort with their commander. General Braddock died along the way and was buried on the road. Braddock's aide, George Washington, was out of a job.

As the British approached Fort Duquesne, they were ambushed by American Indians.

This time, Washington was considered a hero by most colonists and military men. He had showed remarkable courage under fire,

brought his wounded general off the battleground, and led the survivors to safety.

British officials looked at things differently. They blamed the colonial soldiers—including Washington—for the panic and flight at the scene of battle. Washington had done his best to save his soldiers from the French and American Indian attack. Now he became determined never to go back into battle unless he himself was in command.[17]

The Virginia General Assembly created its own small army. It made George Washington, now age twenty-two, "Colonel of the Virginia Regiment and Commander in Chief of all Virginia forces."[18] The

The fatally wounded general Edward Braddock was carried away from battle near Fort Duquesne on a cart.

French and Indian War, as it was known in the colonies, was long and hard. In England it was called the Seven Years' War. Colonel Washington directed the building of a chain of forts along the frontier. He gained a reputation for being personally courageous, though very strict with his men. During some terrible battles, Washington lost one out of every three of his men. And yet his officers were very loyal to him. They threatened to quit if Washington was removed from command.[19]

An End in Sight, and New Beginnings

While Washington was fighting the French and Indian War, he also thought about his own future. He wanted to participate in governing the Virginia colony. In 1758, while he was in Frederick County organizing troops for a final assault on Fort Duquesne, Washington took a step in that direction. He announced that he would run for the House of Burgesses, the Virginia legislature that was elected by the colonists. Even though he had to return to the war front and could not be there to help raise votes, Washington won the election.[20]

Finally, the British brought enough troops into the war to defeat the French. Washington led his Virginia Regiment as part of the forces that captured Fort Duquesne in 1758. The worst threat to the Virginia frontier was gone. Fighting continued in the northern colonies until 1760, but eventually the British triumphed. The war formally ended with a peace treaty in 1763.

A Man of Power

IN 1758, WITH THE DEFEAT of the French at Fort Duquesne, the worst of the French and Indian War was over for Virginia. George Washington felt that he had done his part in defending his country. He resigned his military commission and went home to begin serving in the Virginia House of Burgesses. He began to remodel the Mount Vernon mansion, and he also visited the woman that he had decided to marry.

Martha Custis was a pleasant woman a year or so older than Washington. She had been married to a wealthy plantation owner. Martha and her first husband had had four children, only two of them still living. Martha's husband had died two years earlier. She owned a lot of property. She was friendly, kind, and had a great deal of common sense.[1]

In January 1759, George Washington and Martha Custis were married. The bride was only five feet tall, more than a foot shorter than her husband. The couple settled down together at Mount Vernon. Washington found his wife to be a good companion and "a quiet soul."[2] Indeed, Martha's personality was almost the opposite of Washington's own mother, who had become more and more critical and demanding over the years.[3]

A Country Gentleman at Last

Washington began to enjoy the kind of life he had hoped for as a boy. As a military hero and a member of the Virginia House of Burgesses, he was recognized as an important person in the Virginia colony. He bought fine things for his home and fashionable clothes for himself and

George Washington and Martha Custis were married in January 1759. Washington was twenty-six years old.

Plantations

A plantation is a large estate or farm on which crops are grown. In the southern colonies, early plantations raised tobacco and rice. Later, in the early 1800s, cotton also became an important crop. Most workers on these huge plantations were slaves.

George Washington's plantation, Mount Vernon, consisted of five separate farms and operated like a small town. In addition to producing products to sell, the plantation had to support all who lived there—relatives, overseers, and around three hundred slaves, many of whom were skilled craftsmen. That meant raising thousands of pounds of pork and huge quantities of corn and other grains, catching tens of thousands of fish, and making gallons of cider, wine, and liquor. Washington's workers shod horses, made tools, built barrels, wove fabric, made clothes, raised and trained farm animals, and built and repaired buildings.[4]

Mount Vernon plantation

his family. He gambled at cards. He rode on foxhunts. He bred fine horses.

Washington especially enjoyed seeing plays. Even during his service in the French and Indian War, he had twice managed to see productions in New York City. He went to the theater whenever he could.

Later, he would have plays performed at military camps and at the presidential mansion.[5] He also liked to read. During his lifetime, Washington built up a library of nine hundred books.[6]

The Washingtons attended social occasions, and invited many people to parties at Mount Vernon. Washington invited friends and relatives to visit. He even put up travelers who happened to be passing by. Between 1768 and 1775, he and Martha entertained about two thousand guests.[7]

During this time, Washington bought more land and more slaves. It seems that he had not yet given much thought to moral questions about the existence of slavery. Plantation life was the only desirable way of life he knew, and at that time there was no way to run a plantation without slaves. He did, however, feel a responsibility to treat his slaves well.

Unlike many other plantation owners, Washington came to believe that slaves should not be separated from their families and friends. He would not send a slave away from Mount Vernon unless the slave agreed to the move. He also would not sell slaves just because they got old. That meant that Washington seldom sold any slaves at all.[8]

Although Washington worked hard at managing his property, he soon found himself in debt. The property had been badly run while he was away at war. The buildings had been neglected and repairs seemed endless.[9] It did not help that it was expensive to support his new wife and stepchildren.

Washington changed some of his farming methods. He studied agricultural manuals as he had once studied military manuals. He developed a crop rotation system and planted grasses to help prevent soil erosion. He developed new tools for farming. Instead of only growing tobacco to sell in England, Washington grew wheat and corn that he could sell locally and to island colonies in the Caribbean Sea.[10]

He also changed his business practices. Washington began to buy goods from local importers rather than ordering them directly from England. He was becoming less dependent on the British long before he went to war against them.[11]

In spite of all his efforts, Washington always would have problems with managing the Mount Vernon estate. One reason was that he was so often pulled away from his plantation to take care of larger concerns—colonial problems, and eventually the problems of a new nation.

From Politician Back to Soldier Again

Washington began serving in Virginia's House of Burgesses in 1759, on his twenty-seventh birthday. The famous orator, Patrick Henry, was a member.

Ten years later, Thomas Jefferson also became a Burgess. The Burgesses were called into session whenever the Virginia governor needed their vote on any matter. To most members, being a Burgess meant little more than an occasional interruption of their normal lives. No one yet realized that the House

Washington would always have financial problems with the Mount Vernon plantation.

of Burgesses was bringing together some of the men who would lead America to independence from Great Britain.

After the French and Indian War, which had been very expensive, Great Britain imposed new taxes on the colonies to help pay its bills. Rather than returning home, many of the British military forces stayed in America to protect the frontiers. The colonists began to feel that their rights as British citizens were being ignored. By 1769, Washington was getting worried about British behavior, and even visualized the possibility of an armed rebellion, but only as a last resort.[12]

George Washington thought that the Boston Tea Party was a mistake.[13] He was sure that it

The Boston Tea Party

On December 16, 1773, angry Bostonians protested the British tax on tea imported to the colonies. The

colonists dressed up as American Indians and raided three ships in the Boston harbor. They broke open 342 chests of British tea and dumped the tea overboard. So much tea was thrown into the water that it piled up in little islands.

would only drive the British to greater extremes. Washington was right about that. The British made a series of new laws that colonists called the "Intolerable Acts." The British closed the Boston harbor. They said that the citizens of Massachusetts could not hold town meetings without permission. The British also gave some western territory claimed by Massachusetts, Connecticut, and Virginia to Canada. And all the colonies were ordered to help provide food and housing for the British soldiers.

In the fall of 1774, the colonies sent delegates to Philadelphia to discuss the situation. Washington and six other Virginians attended the meeting, which was the First Continental Congress. The delegates aired their complaints against

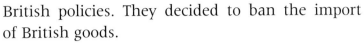

British policies. They decided to ban the import of British goods.

While in Philadelphia, Washington agreed that refusing to buy anything from England was the best form of protest. But back in Virginia, he drilled the militia to be ready for battle.[14]

After the battles at Lexington and Concord, the Second Continental Congress met in Philadelphia,

The Revolution's Earliest Battles

In April 1775, troops from the Massachusetts colony fought with the British at Lexington and Concord. The colonial troops pursued the British army to Boston, inflicting many casualties. Although the British seized Boston, the Massachusetts troops, joined by militiamen from other nearby New England colonies, kept the city surrounded.

The first major battle was at Boston in June 1775. It became known as the Battle of Bunker Hill (although it was actually fought on nearby Breed's Hill). The British finally won the hill, but the victory cost them more than a thousand casualties.

British general Thomas Gage

After these early fights, British general Thomas Gage realized that colonial soldiers might be amateurs, but they would be hard to beat. He wrote to his superiors that England must either send large armies to fight the colonists or give up the colonies. Gage's warnings were ignored.

with John Hancock as president. They created the Continental army to oppose the British. Most colonists, including Washington, were still not seeking independence from England. They wanted to use military action to force England to compromise on colonial problems.

John Adams knew that if militiamen from various colonies were to work together in a single army, they would need a strong leader. Adams thought that George Washington would be the perfect man for the job. Partly at Adams's urging, George Washington was appointed Commander in Chief of the Continental army.

Washington had been happy living at Mount Vernon and knew that he would miss the comforts of home. He was filled with doubts about his ability to do the job. But he did not feel that he could turn down this call to duty. Washington accepted the post, but he told Congress "my abilities . . . may not be equal to the extensive and important Trust." He confided to his brother-in-law that he feared his lack of experience might be fatal.[15]

The General and the American Revolution

DURING HIS EARLIER MILITARY service in the French and Indian War, George Washington had studied British military manuals. He had seen first-hand how the British preferred to fight. He had also learned different fighting tactics from the American Indians he fought with and against.

During his years at Mount Vernon, Washington thought a lot about what made a good military leader.[1] He realized that a commander must know how to deal with different kinds of men. He believed that a good officer sometimes had to be severe. He felt that it was more important to win admiration than friendship.[2] When he was made general and put in command of the Continental army, Washington had the appearance and the mind of a leader. But at first, there was no actual Continental army for him to command.

The New England militias had fought the British several times, including during the Battle of Bunker Hill. In the militia, men elected their officers and expected to have a vote on all matters.[3] Would these disorderly but successful fighters take orders from a stranger from another colony?

In June 1775, General Washington joined the New England army in Massachusetts. He soon discovered that he had far fewer men and supplies than Congress had promised him. The men he did have were undisciplined. Washington began at once to set things straight. He insisted that the men dig proper privies (latrines) to prevent disease. He planned a system of trenches and fortifications and set the men to work on them. He demoted several officers and taught the others to behave like leaders rather than like ordinary soldiers.

George Washington studied British military manuals during his early career as a soldier. Artist Charles Wilson Peale painted forty-year-old Washington in his Virginia military uniform in 1772. This is the first portrait ever made of Washington.

Some men who refused Washington's orders were whipped.

The New Englanders appreciated certain things about General Washington—that he refused to accept any pay, for example. Many were glad to see discipline brought to the Continental army.[4] And they appreciated the fact that Washington stayed right with his men during their reorganization and retraining.

When the Continental Congress tried to lower military pay, Washington and his officers stood together to make Congress back down.[5] The Continental army began to grow with new enlisted soldiers from many colonies.

Fighting Against the British

Washington was proud of his men for holding their ground outside Boston. Still, the Continental army had not yet met the British forces in battle. Washington expected that the departing British ships and troops would move to New York City, and he transferred his army from Boston to that area.

After the transfer, Washington went to Philadelphia to request more troops and supplies from the Continental Congress. He found Congress about to make a bold move. They were talking about declaring America's independence from England. By then, Washington agreed that they should do so.[6] But he did not believe that the military should interfere in political decisions, so he said nothing publicly about independence.

The Boston Compromise

In 1775, British troops still held Boston, but the colonists had Boston surrounded. Washington wanted to attack and take back the city. But the Continental Congress was afraid that American losses would be too great. Washington was, then and always, careful to respect the will of Congress. So instead of attacking, Washington increased the fortifications around the city.

Three thousand American soldiers climbed the hills around Boston, dug trenches in the frozen earth, and set up a cannon that had been captured from the British. When the British commander saw the cannon, he offered Washington a deal—let the British troops out, and the British would not destroy the city. Washington would have preferred to fight, but he agreed to the deal in order to save Boston.[7]

When the British army left Boston in March 1776, they got into their ships and sailed out of sight, headed for Halifax, Nova Scotia.

Washington was back with his army when British ships loaded with troops arrived at New York harbor. A few days later, on July 6, 1776, he received a copy of the Declaration of Independence. When he had it read to his troops, some cheered. But Washington was not sure how many of them were really happy at suddenly being American rather than British citizens.[8] Then, some of his soldiers demonstrated their enthusiasm by joining a civilian mob. They pulled down a huge metal statue of the British king and tore off its head. Washington had to reprimand them for their "want of order."[9]

More and more British ships arrived in New York harbor, carrying more and more British soldiers. The harbor was cluttered with the spiky masts of British ships. The British had about thirty thousand well-trained soldiers camped on Staten Island. Some were German and Hessian professional military men.

Although the Continental army was in much better shape than when Washington first took command, the twenty-three thousand American troops were still only partially-trained. America could easily have lost the war in those first battles. Compared to the British, Washington and his men were terribly inexperienced. More than once, Washington charged his horse toward the battle line, only to find himself surrounded by his own soldiers—running away.[10] Washington's military plans often failed, and he lost a lot of equipment and cannons in his early battles against the British.

Fortunately for the Americans, British general William Howe was reluctant to lose many men after suffering so many casualties at the Battle of Bunker Hill. It was very expensive to bring in new professional soldiers from England—three thousand miles across the ocean. So the British did not attack Washington head-on. Instead, they used their ships to move men around and make surprise attacks.

In August 1776, the British landed on Long Island and cornered more than nine thousand American soldiers in Brooklyn. New York's East River was full of British battleships, with cannons that could fire on the Americans. And about twenty thousand British troops were marching westward across Long Island toward the Americans stationed there. In a series of attacks, many Americans were killed or captured. General Howe paused to see if the Americans would give up.

Fortunately for the Americans, a cold, foggy rain swept in, making both armies invisible. The British ships and soldiers stayed in place, waiting for the fog to lift. The next morning, to the amazement of General Howe, the American troops were gone. Washington had secretly rounded up every small boat he could find. When the fog moved in, he and his men rowed away to Manhattan Island. They escaped the British, but after a series of battles and retreats in the following days, Washington abandoned New York City to the British.

The British had been trained to fight in tight military formations, working together as a group. Washington knew that his men could not fight that way. He started using hit-and-run tactics, striking and quickly retreating. But Washington hated running like a hunted fox.[11] By the end of 1776, Washington and his army were retreating across New Jersey.

Although the Continental army was surviving, it was not winning many battles. That drove more and more soldiers and civilians to switch to the British side. Washington's spirits sank, and he wrote, "I think the game is pretty near up."[12]

In December 1776, Washington and his troops had been forced back to the Delaware River. The men were cold and hungry, and many of them were ill. Washington took his troops across to the Pennsylvania side. To keep the British from following, Washington took every boat he could find with him.

As the British army drew near the Delaware River, the Continental Congress fled from Philadelphia. But instead of bringing in new boats and attacking, the British turned back. Faced with snow and freezing weather, the British returned to their winter quarters in New York. They left a guard of two to three thousand Hessian soldiers camped at Trenton, New Jersey.[13]

What remained of the Continental army was safe for the moment, but General George Washington was furious. He was tired of begging Congress to send badly needed supplies and funds. He was tired of retreating, of being "pushed . . . from place to place."[14] Even worse, two officers he had put in charge of other army divisions were not following his orders. He learned that they were openly questioning his ability to command. Washington needed a victory.

The Delaware River was filled with floating chunks of ice, but it was not frozen over. Washington still had the boats he had collected to keep the British from crossing. Now, he would use those boats himself—but not to run away. He would make a desperate, seemingly impossible, surprise attack on the enemy.

On Christmas Day, 1776, Washington set out with 2,400 men.[15] He only got about a third of them across the river before a freezing storm moved in. The rest could not cross. Those who had made the trip had to march another nine miles through ice and snow. Those who stopped to rest risked freezing to death right where they were.[16] Washington and his troops arrived at the Hessian camp after dawn on December 26. Snow was coming down hard.

Washington Crossing the Delaware *shows George Washington taking his troops to attack the enemy by surprise. The crossing—made during a winter storm— was probably much more difficult than it appears in this copy of an 1851 painting by Emanuel Leutz.*

The Hessians never expected an attack in such a storm. After a party the night before, they were barely awake.[17] In the driving snow, the Hessians could not see well enough to get into military formation. Unable to fight any other way, the Hessians soon surrendered.[18]

Crossing the Delaware brought Washington his first great victory of the war. He had proved that a sudden surprise move could beat the British.[19] The next battle, at Princeton, New Jersey, on January 3, 1777, was brief and hard. This time it was the British who broke and ran.

Washington's military success began to attract attention at home and abroad. With new hopes for victory, Congress finally agreed to pay for a more professional army. The men enlisted for longer terms. The French were impressed enough to start sending weapons to the Americans.

After the victories at Princeton and Trenton, Washington withdrew his army to Morristown, New Jersey, for the winter of 1777. Finally, it was simply too cold to fight. In the battles that followed that year, both American and British troops suffered heavy losses. Washington won some battles, but he never defeated the main British army. Reinforcements that Washington ordered up did not arrive. Some of his generals still did not obey his orders. The British occupied Philadelphia in September 1777, and Washington could not find a way to get them out.

Shocked by Washington's attack, the Hessian troops soon surrendered.
Surrender of Hessian Troops to General Washington, after Battle of
Trenton, December 1776 *is a copy of an 1850 lithograph.*

Starving and Freezing

Following the loss of Philadelphia, Washington
decided to build his winter camp for 1777–1778 at
Valley Forge, Pennsylvania, rather than impose on
any of the towns near Philadelphia. During the
first two months in that winter camp, the soldiers
lived in rough tents until they could build cabins
with fireplaces. The men were barely clothed, and
many did not have shoes.

Nobody knows how many American soldiers
died that winter from the cold and from diseases
such as smallpox. Estimates run from just under

a thousand to more than three thousand. Every day, a dozen or so men deserted.[20] But within two months, conditions had improved a little. The cabins were finished, and food was in better supply. The men in each cabin joked that they could get enough clothes together for one roommate at a time to go out for rations.[21]

Washington knew that although the American troops had improved, they still needed training to compete with their enemy's professional soldiers. He welcomed the help of a volunteer officer named Friederich von Steuben, who claimed to have held a high military rank in Germany. Although that turned out to be untrue, Steuben proved to be an excellent military trainer. He taught the Americans how to fight in military formation, like the British did. Washington's troops were soon competing with each other to perfect Steuben's drills.[22] When Washington left Valley

Washington and his army had another victory against the British at Princeton, New Jersey. Washington at Princeton Jany.3rd, 1777 *is a copy of a lithograph by D. McLellan.*

There comes a soldier, his bare feet are seen thro' his worn out Shoes, his legs nearly naked from the tatter'd remains of an only pair of stockings, his Breeches not sufficient to cover his nakedness, his Shirt hanging in Strings, his hair dishevell'd. . . . He comes and crys . . . I am Sick, my feet lame, my legs are sore, my body cover'd with this tormenting Itch. . . . I fail fast I shall soon be no more! and all the reward I shall get will be—"Poor Will is dead."[23]

A camp surgeon wrote about the suffering of a soldier at Washington's Valley Forge winter camp.

Forge in the spring, he had a much better-trained fighting force.

In June 1778, Washington's spies—the local washerwomen—told him that British officers in Philadelphia wanted their laundry delivered at once, regardless of whether it was finished.[24] Washington realized what that meant. The British had decided it was pointless to continue occupying Philadelphia and were going to abandon the city.

Washington caught up with the British at Monmouth Courthouse, New Jersey. In the battle that followed, some soldiers collapsed from the hundred-degree heat. One of Washington's generals retreated with his men, instead of attacking. It looked like Washington might lose his entire army.[25] But as he had often done before, Washington rode among his troops, calling them back to action.

Washington's aide, a young man named Alexander Hamilton, wrote that Washington "by his own presence . . . brought order out of confusion."[26] A French ally on Washington's staff, the Marquis de Lafayette, was even more impressed. Lafayette described how Washington

> seemed to arrest fortune with one glance. . . . His presence stopped the retreat. . . . His graceful bearing on horseback, his calm and deportment which still retained a trace of displeasure . . . were all calculated to inspire the highest degree of enthusiasm. . . . I thought then as now that I had never beheld so superb a man.[27]

When the American soldiers used the formations they had learned during the terrible winter, they drove the British back.

The British retreated behind their fortifications at New York City. They had expected a quick victory, but after two years of fighting, they were right back where they had started.[28] But Washington was also facing serious problems. The Continental Congress was sending less money than ever, and some Continental soldiers were threatening to mutiny. Fortunately, in early 1778, the French had officially joined the American cause, contributing troops, supplies, and a navy.

Victory at Yorktown

As the war dragged on, the British turned their attention to the southern states. In the south, they hoped to find more Americans who were loyal to Great Britain. At first, the British were successful. They captured Savannah, Georgia, in December 1778, and gradually moved north toward Virginia.

The Americans would not give up. Troops under General Nathanael Greene attacked the British army in North and South Carolina. British general Charles Cornwallis turned his attention to Virginia in 1781. The state's governor, Thomas Jefferson, fled his home for a while. In August, Cornwallis moved his troops to Yorktown, on the Chesapeake Bay, to establish his headquarters at a place with easy access to the British navy for support and supplies.

On August 14, 1781, Washington received word that a new French fleet was on its way with more than three thousand soldiers to support the American cause.[29] But the ships would not come to New York City, where Washington and his army were camped nearby. Instead, they would head for the Chesapeake Bay, 450 miles to the south.

If French ships were really coming, Washington could attack Cornwallis with their help. But to do that, Washington would have to move a large number of soldiers south fast, and without the British realizing what he was doing.

Washington knew that British spies surrounded him, so he tricked them. He leaked supposedly secret papers that said the French were coming to fight in New York. At the same time, Washington built a fake army camp in New Jersey. The British were fooled. Washington was able to slip away with 2,500 men.[30] On the way south, he was joined by a larger number of French troops under the command of French general Jean-Baptiste Donatien de Vimeur, Comte de Rochambeau.

The exhausted and ragged American soldiers marched southward along-side their well-dressed French allies. At the same time, Rochambeau and his

In The Surrender of Lord Cornwallis at Yorktown *by John Trumbull, the man on the white horse is not George Washington. Because Cornwallis refused to attend the surrender ceremony, Washington sent his second in command, General Benjamin Lincoln, to accept the surrender. Washington is on a dark horse near the American flag.*

staff sailed down the Delaware River by boat. On the Pennsylvania waterfront, Rochambeau saw a tall man in uniform dancing up and down and waving at them from a wharf. It was George Washington, who had received news that the French fleet actually had arrived. Washington was delighted and even hugged Rochambeau when the two men actually met.[31]

Cornwallis thought that his British troops were secure behind the excellent fortifications they had built at Yorktown. But soon, Cornwallis found himself in serious trouble. Besides the eight

George Washington made a farewell speech to his officers when he retired from the army in 1783.

$\mathcal{A}$ contemplation of the compleat attainment (at a period earlier than could have been expected) of the object for which we contended against so formidable a power cannot but inspire us with astonishment and gratitude. The ... unparalleled perseverence of the Armies of the U States, through almost every possible suffering and discouragement for the space of eight long years, was little short of a standing miracle. ...

Every American Officer and Soldier must now console himself for any unpleasant circumstances which may have occurred by a recollection of the uncommon scenes in which he has been called to Act ... and the astonishing events of which he has been a witness, events which have seldom if ever before taken place on the stage of human action, nor can they probably ever happen again. For who has before seen a disciplined Army form'd at once from such raw materials? Who, that was not a witness, could imagine that the most violent local prejudices would cease so soon, and that Men who came from the different parts of the Continent, strongly disposed, by the habits of education, to despise and quarrel with each other, would instantly become but one patriotic band of Brothers ...[32]

In his farewell address to the army, Washington congratulated his men on the victories they had won over themselves, as well as over the enemy.

thousand French troops in ships and on the shore, Americans had flocked from the countryside to join General Washington. The French naval fleet drove the British ships from the Chesapeake Bay, preventing Cornwallis from retreating or receiving help. On October 17, after a three-week siege and bombardment of Yorktown, Cornwallis proposed a truce to work out terms for the surrender.

The defeat of Cornwallis was the final major battle of the American Revolution, but not the final problem. As peace talks went on in Paris, Washington had to keep his troops together and fully disciplined, even though they were not being paid. This is what led to the challenge from his officers at Newburgh, New York. On November 25, 1783, the British left New York City. On December 4, General Washington made a farewell speech to his officers. He retired from the army—and from public life, or so he thought.

From Confusion to a Constitution

IN PAINTINGS OF General George Washington, he is often shown riding a great white horse. Actually, Washington's favorite battle horse was a sorrel (reddish color) named Nelson.[1] Another of his warhorses was a gray named Blueskin.

In 1783, George Washington hoped that he, like his horses, could retire to Mount Vernon. He looked forward to living the life of a country gentleman again. He wanted to study history and perhaps French. Washington realized that he was a famous man, but he still thought that he could lead a quiet life at home.[2]

Of course, nothing was quite the same. His old friend, George William Fairfax, and his wife, Sally, had moved to England. The Fairfax plantation

When dinner was over, we visited the General's stables, saw his magnificent horses, among them "Old Nelson," now twenty-two years of age, that carried the General almost always during the war. "Blueskin," another fine old horse, next to him, had that honor. They had heard the roaring of many a cannon in their time. . . . The General makes no manner of use of them now. He keeps them in a nice stable, where they feed away at their ease for their past services.[3]

In a letter to a friend, an English visitor to Mount Vernon described two of Washington's horses and their services during the American Revolution.

house, Belvoir, had been burned during the war. Far from being quiet, Mount Vernon was constantly full of people. They came to visit from all the states, from France, and even from England.[4] In addition to visitors, letters poured in. Washington thought that every letter deserved an answer, but he had to hire a secretary to help with them.

When George Washington's mother wrote to complain that her famous son was neglecting her,

Washington suggested that she sell the house he had given her and move in with some other family member. Mount Vernon, he hastened to add, would be far too noisy and crowded for her taste.[5]

In spite of all the demands on his attention, Washington's main occupation was the management of his plantation. Every morning except Sunday, he rode around his entire Mount Vernon property.[6] But Washington did not get to retire from public life. He had only been home a few years when new and serious national problems arose. The United States needed a more effective national government.

One Nation—or Thirteen?

In the Declaration of Independence, the thirteen colonies called themselves the United States of America. That did not mean what it does today. Originally, the states acted like separate small nations. Most people thought of themselves as citizens of a particular state rather than one big nation.

In paintings, Washington is often shown dramatically posed on a proud white horse.

When the Revolutionary War was over, the states were eager to hold on to their own power. Even though they had joined together to defeat a common enemy, the states had a hard time cooperating on much of anything else. The Continental Congress continued to vote for money to keep the national army going, in case it was needed. But the individual states continued to ignore requests for money made by Congress.

The First Constitution

The Continental Congress declared independence from Great Britain in 1776. In 1777, Congress drafted the Articles of Confederation, describing how the new country would be run. After much discussion, Congress finally approved the Articles in 1781. Like the Declaration of Independence, the Articles referred to the United Sates of America. But the Articles described this as a "league of friendship" to handle issues like "common defense."

The Articles said that citizens—except for "paupers, vagabonds, and fugitives from justice"—could come and go freely from state to state without losing their rights. The Articles gave Congress the power to declare war, make treaties, settle boundary disputes, establish a national money system, establish a postal service, and perform some other normal duties of a central government.

For a governing body, the Articles of Confederation created one branch of government—the legislative or law-making branch of Congress. The Articles did not establish a judicial branch, which would have led to a system of courts. It did not create an executive branch, which would have included a chief executive, or president. No one in national office received a salary. Each state could have up to seven representatives in Congress, but each state had only one vote.

Some important things were left out of the Articles of Confederation. The central government could not tax anyone to raise money. Congress had to ask the states for any money it needed. All important decisions—such as whether to obey national laws or to give Congress any money—were left up to each individual state.

Any changes in the Articles of Confederation had to be approved by all thirteen states. Some amendments were proposed, but not a single one ever passed.

A Nation in Trouble

Some states were willing to work together on particular problems. In March 1785, representatives from Virginia and Maryland met to talk about making the Potomac River easier to navigate. The following year, Virginia invited all thirteen states to send representatives to a similar meeting in Annapolis, Maryland. But by the time the Annapolis meeting took place, the new nation was obviously in trouble.

In September 1786, five states sent delegates to the Annapolis Convention. George Washington did

Shays's Rebellion

By summer 1786, many farmers in western Massachusetts owed money on their property. There was no way they could earn enough money to pay their debts. The Massachusetts government began to seize their farms. Some farm owners were thrown into prison because of their debts.

A mob led by a Revolutionary War veteran named Daniel Shays began to break into courtrooms and stop trials. His followers destroyed courthouse records. They raided prisons and set debtors free. They even tried to seize weapons stored in an arsenal at Springfield. It took the Massachusetts militia to stop them. The leaders of Shays's Rebellion

not attend in person, but he let his opinion be known. He thought that the delegates should not limit their discussions to economic problems. The delegates agreed. In their report to the Continental Congress and to state legislatures, they called for another meeting to discuss the problems of the United States.

There were some familiar problems and some new ones. The army veterans Washington had talked to at Newburgh, New York, had still not received all that they had been promised by Congress. Now, the states were in deep financial trouble. To pay their debts, some states taxed their citizens heavily, and some printed large amounts of worthless paper money.

were caught, tried, and sentenced to death. But public sympathy was with the rebels, and they were pardoned.

Even so, Shays's Rebellion convinced many of the nation's leaders—including Washington—that the new nation needed a change in government. The American experiment could possibly fail without a stronger central government.

The mob during Shays's Rebellion

Shays's Rebellion frightened many political leaders. They knew that the country had no way to fix the farmers' problems or to put down a revolt. In case of a major rebellion, nobody knew who might end up running a state, or even the entire country.[7]

In March 1787, the Continental Congress called for a Federal Convention of delegates to "be held at Philadelphia for the sole and express purpose of revising the Articles of Confederation." The resolution did not say anything about writing a whole new constitution, but that is what happened. The Federal Convention would become known as the Constitutional Convention.

Compromises for a Constitution

The Federal Convention was scheduled to begin on May 14, 1787, but many delegates were not there by that date. While they waited for the rest to arrive, George Washington, James Madison, and others from Virginia worked on their ideas. When the meeting began, Virginia governor Edmund Randolph presented the Virginia Plan. Madison had written it, and it was very different from the Articles of Confederation.

Many delegates realized for the first time that they were not there just to fix the Articles of Confederation. They were going to do something much more daring and not strictly legal. According to the Articles of Confederation, any changes required the approval of every state legislature. To get around that, the delegates to the Federal Convention simply scrapped the Articles and started over. They were going to create a completely new form of government, unlike any seen before.

First, the delegates unanimously elected George Washington president of the convention. As president, Washington did not take part in the formal discussions. But he still showed his agreement, anger, or boredom.[8] Many years later, Jonathan Dayton of New Jersey described Washington during one debate. At one point, "the countenance of Washington brightened," but at another, "Washington fixed his eye upon the speaker with a mixture of surprise and indignation."[9] After hours, Washington was anything but silent. His lively opinions were heard at social events, between the acts of plays, and at gatherings in local taverns.

The Virginia Plan called for a government with three branches—legislative, executive, and judicial. The legislative branch of government would have two houses. Although that was very much like the new state governments, many questions still had to be settled. Throughout the sweltering heat of a Philadelphia summer, the delegates worked in great secrecy. They were forbidden to discuss what they were doing with outsiders. Today, people only know what happened because James Madison took excellent notes. The delegates argued some of the major points—and ended up compromising to reach a solution.

At the time of the Constitutional Convention, Charles Wilson Peale painted this portrait of George Washington.

How many votes would each state have? If the number was based on a state's population, the small states would never be heard. If each state had the same number of votes, large numbers of people in the big states would have no more say than small numbers of people in the small states. The delegates reached a compromise just in time to keep the convention from ending in failure. The two houses of Congress would be set up differently. Each state would have two Senators, but the number of members in the House of Representatives would depend on a state's population.

Would slavery be outlawed? Some delegates, including George Washington, had come to believe that slavery was not right. Some northern states had already outlawed slavery. But the southern states insisted that slavery was absolutely necessary to their economy. It became obvious that if Congress tried to outlaw slavery, the country was going to split into two nations. One nation would be made up of states that held slaves, and the other of states that did not. If that happened, slavery would still not be abolished, but the union would be lost.

Washington felt that it was important to first strengthen the bond among the states. Perhaps then a strong central government would be able to abolish slavery. Congress decided not to outlaw slavery. They also allowed the importation of slaves to continue until 1808.

How would a state's population be counted? States with slaves wanted to count them in the population, even though the slaves did not have the rights of citizens and could not vote. Counting slaves would give the slave-owning states more representatives in Congress. After much argument, the delegates agreed that a state could count three-fifths of their slaves as part of their population for both representation and taxation.

The new Constitution gave Congress the power to tax, coin money, establish the courts, and provide for the "general welfare of the United States."[10] The Constitution also included ways to make changes in the document itself.

To prevent any one branch of government from taking all the power, the Constitution set up a system of checks and balances. For example, bills had to be approved by both houses of Congress and also signed by the president. The president was to be Commander in Chief of the armed forces, but only Congress could declare war.

On September 17, Congress was ready to vote on the Constitution. Nobody was completely happy with all the compromises. Benjamin Franklin, who was eighty-two and very weak, wrote out a speech for another delegate to read. "I agree to this Constitution with all its faults, if they are such; because I think a general Government necessary for us."[11] Franklin pointed out that he had lived a long time, had learned from others, and had often had to change his own opinion. He thought that the Constitution was the best they could do, and appealed to the other delegates to approve and sign it.

Delegates from twelve states signed the document that day. (Rhode Island did not send delegates to the convention.) Now, the Constitution had to be ratified (approved) by at least nine states. Alexander Hamilton, James Madison, and John Jay published essays in favor of ratification, now known as *The Federalist*.

In letters to several Virginia leaders, Washington said that he wished the "Constitution which is offered had been made more perfect, but I sincerely believe it is the best that could be obtained at this time."[12] He also pointed out that it could be amended.

In June 1788, the state of Virginia became the tenth state to ratify the Constitution. Eventually all thirteen states accepted it. James Monroe, a young delegate from Virginia and future president, wrote to Thomas Jefferson about George Washington, saying, "Be assured, his influence carried this government."[13]

The First President

UNDER THE ARTICLES OF CONFEDERATION, the United States had been run by the Continental Congress, which acted as a large committee. The new Constitution divided up the government's responsibilities. Now the main person in charge was to be a president, but nobody was sure exactly what he was supposed to do. No government had ever been set up this way before.

Most countries, including Spain and France, still had absolute monarchies. In those countries, a king or queen inherited the job and ruled—with few questions allowed. England still had a king, but it also had Parliament, an elected legislature whose members represented the people. By the 1780s, Parliament had gained enough power to put some limits on the king's decisions. This system was called constitutional monarchy.

Some Americans said that constitutional monarchy was right for the United States. The new country still had many problems to solve, and a few thought that only a king could keep it from falling apart.[1] Other Americans were very anxious to keep their new country from becoming any kind of monarchy. As British citizens, they had already lived under that system. As American citizens, they wanted to have more personal say about how the country was run. They saw the president as a completely new kind of leader. He should hold a certain amount of power, but that power should be limited, and he should not have it for life.

Most citizens of the new country did not have much trouble imagining who would be president. Benjamin Franklin would have been a possible choice if he had not been too old to lead. There was no doubt in most minds that Washington was the right man for the job.

The Man for the Job

George Washington always had an impressive physical presence. When he became president, he was a tall, slender, imposing, and graceful man. John Adams's wife, Abigail, was not easily impressed, but when she met Washington she wrote to her husband that Washington moved "with a grace, dignity, and ease that leaves [the king of England] far behind him."[2]

The members of Congress knew that Washington had never tried to hold onto power for himself. He would have considered such behavior as dishonorable. Throughout history, great military leaders have often become tyrannical rulers.[3] But after winning on the battlefield, Washington had simply retired from the military.[4]

Washington already had learned a lot of things that a national leader needed to know. He had traveled to many parts of the country and had seen the differences in attitudes and economic conditions. He already knew many of the men who were now leaders in Congress. He understood the concerns of the people very well.

When the first electors voted on February 4, 1789, they unanimously elected Washington the first president. John Adams became vice president. There was plenty of doubt in George Washington's mind about accepting the presidency. He preferred

Electing a President

During the Constitutional Convention, some delegates wanted the president to be elected by the people, but others wanted him to be chosen by the state legislatures. The delegates had compromised by creating an electoral college. Each state could appoint as many electors as they had representatives and senators combined, and a state could select its electors however it wanted to. The electors would then vote to decide who would be president.

retirement. Besides, he was not sure if he would be up to the job. Even so, Alexander Hamilton and other influential men persuaded Washington that he could not refuse his duty. The country, they insisted, could not do without him.

Then, there was a problem of his official title. The word "president" is based on French and Latin words meaning someone who presides or stands guard. The title had been used for the head officer of a colony and for the leader of the Continental Congress. But was it suitable for the chief executive of a republic? Did it have the proper grandeur?

Washington was horrified when a group of senators, led by John Adams, suggested, "His Highness, the President of the United States of America, and Protector of Their Liberties."[5] At Washington's request, Virginia representative James Madison encouraged the House of Representatives to insist on a simpler title, "Mr. President." Fortunately, the Senate agreed.[6]

When George Washington traveled from Virginia to New York City for his inauguration, cheering crowds and celebrations greeted him all along the way. On April 30, 1789, Washington was inaugurated the first president of the United States.

How to Begin?

Washington knew very well that he was setting an example for all presidents who would come after him. He wrote, "I walk on Untrodden ground.

George Washington took the oath of office as the president of the United States on April 30, 1789.

There is scarcely any part of my conduct which may not hereafter be drawn into precedent."[7]

During Washington's first term, he dealt with various domestic matters. For example, the Constitution suggested that there would be heads of departments, which we now call Cabinet members. Washington organized the first Cabinet, which included Thomas Jefferson as secretary of state and Alexander Hamilton as secretary of the treasury.

This is a copy of George Washington's first inaugural address—and the first for the United States.

While in his first term, George Washington also encouraged the states to accept the Constitution, reminding them that it could be improved later. In September 1789, Congress recommended twelve amendments to the Constitution. The states ratified ten of these by December 1791. These ten are known as the Bill of Rights.

Political Parties

The Constitution did not say anything about political parties, and President Washington thought they would be bad for the country. He believed that educated and capable men could work out their differences in a dignified manner without forming parties. But bitter disagreements soon developed between Thomas Jefferson and Alexander Hamilton, both members of Washington's Cabinet.

Jefferson and his followers believed that people could rule themselves without much government interference. They were afraid that too much central power might

Henry Knox (seated) was Washington's secretary of war. Standing are (from left to right) Secretary of State Thomas Jefferson, Attorney General Edmund Randolph, and Secretary of the Treasury Alexander Hamilton.

result in a monarchy. They eventually became known as Republicans.

Hamilton and his followers believed that people needed the protection of a strong government. His group called themselves Federalists, a term that had earlier been used to mean supporters of the Constitution.

Washington agreed with Hamilton more often than he did with Jefferson, but he never identified with either political party. He thought that the correct answers to most important questions lay beneath such surface differences. He constantly wrote letters to supporters on both sides, urging them to compromise.[8]

More than ever, Washington felt overwhelmed with people who came to visit, socialize, or complain. And at first, Martha Washington was not happy about moving to New York, but she learned to handle the constant entertaining that was required of her.

Second Term as President

By the end of his first term, Washington was preparing his retirement speech. But again his associates insisted that the country still needed him. Reluctantly, Washington agreed not to withdraw his name, and in 1793, the electors again voted unanimously for him. More serious challenges arose during his second term.

The French Revolution

In 1789, French peasants began to protest heavy taxes and other social problems. They were supported by French intellectuals, who believed that the monarchy and other privileged groups should sacrifice for the good of the country. In 1792, mobs of people overthrew the royalists.

To Americans, it seemed at first like the French were fighting for the same ideals that the Americans had in their own revolution. But soon, stories of a reign of terror reached the United States. Thousands of people were beheaded in Paris, including the French king and queen.

When France declared war on Great Britain in 1793, Americans were divided over which country to support. Washington had seen enough war and destruction. He was determined that the United States stay neutral in any European conflict.

Other Challenges

In 1790, Congress had put a tax on the sale of whiskey, but many western farmers objected, and some Pennsylvanians refused to pay. Washington knew that if he allowed any group to disregard the law, the government could lose its power. In 1794, the opposition became violent, and Washington called out nearly thirteen thousand state militiamen to restore order. The farmers gave up and agreed to pay the tax. This episode became known as the Whiskey Rebellion.[9]

In 1793, yellow fever broke out in Philadelphia, at that time the capital of the United States. No one knew that mosquitoes carried the disease. The city was sealed off, and Washington carried on government business from Mount Vernon.[10]

Limiting His Terms

By the end of his second term, Washington was tired of political life. He was also afraid that if he continued in office until he died, it would set a bad precedent for future presidents. He absolutely refused to run for a third term. In his Farewell Address on September 17, 1796, Washington reminded his countrymen that they had created the United States together, through collaboration and compromise.

A Hero's Final Years

WASHINGTON WAS THE FIRST ex-president of the United States of America in 1797. During his two terms as president, he had seen the country off to a good start. America had a sound financial system. The new states of Kentucky, Tennessee, and Vermont had been established. Although Washington was not happy that American politicians had divided into two parties, at least both parties supported the existence of a national government.

Avoiding as many ceremonies and celebrations as he could, Washington returned to Mount Vernon.

In Need of Repair

While he was president, Washington often spent his own money on the presidential residence, where he met with congressmen, citizens, and representatives from other nations. Meanwhile, those he left in charge of Mount Vernon had let the plantation run down.

Washington set about having repairs made to his house and getting his plantation operating efficiently.[1] As usual, Washington got up at dawn, and he expected his workmen to do the same. In his journal, Washington described how he spent his days:

> If my hirelings are not in their places at that time, I send them messages expressive of my sorrow for their indisposition. Then, having put these wheels in motion, I examine the state of things further. . . . This over, I mount my horse and ride round my farms, which employs me until it is time to dress for dinner.[2]

After dinner, Washington would take a walk and have a cup of tea. Then, he sometimes answered letters by candlelight. He said, "I have not looked into a book since I came home."[3] He would have no time for reading until the repair work was finished.

The entire property needed as much attention as the house. Mount Vernon was made up of five farms, a total of eight thousand acres. Despite all their crops and livestock, the farms had never produced enough income to satisfy Washington. Now, his financial situation was even worse.[4] Fortunately, some payments were still coming in from property he had sold over the past few years.

During his final years, Washington was often lonely. He was accustomed to the companionship of people discussing important issues. Now, many of his former neighbors had moved away or died. Younger Virginians were mostly followers of Thomas Jefferson, who was often at odds with Washington.[5] Washington did have many visitors, but they were not always especially welcome. He commented that when he came to dinner, "I rarely miss seeing strange faces, come, as they say, out of respect to me. Pray, would not the word curiosity answer as well?"[6] This was very different, Washington added, from having a few friends over for a cheerful meal.

Washington did not completely lose touch with what was going on in the government. He corresponded with the new president, John Adams, and with some of his former Cabinet members who were still in office. In 1798, Washington even accepted command of the army again when war with France seemed likely. But he said he would stay at Mount Vernon unless there was an actual invasion. The threat faded, and Washington did not have to leave home.

Slavery

George Washington had been raised to admire and enjoy plantation life, which was supported by slave labor. During the Revolutionary War, Washington had longed to return to the life of a plantation owner. But he had also begun to doubt both the morality and the practicality of slavery.[7]

For Washington, beliefs and behavior could not be separated. Once he started questioning slavery, he was already on a path leading away from it. He was not able to overcome all the obstacles on that path during his lifetime. But of all the Virginian founding fathers who owned slaves, he became the only one to free all his slaves.[8]

Since before the Revolution, Washington had refused to break up slave families or to sell slaves without their consent. When he returned to Mount Vernon after being president, he had far too many slaves for any farming he was likely to do.[9] He wrote to a relative:

> To sell the overplus I cannot, because I am principled against this kind of traffic in the human species. To hire them out, is almost as bad, because they could not be disposed of in families to any advantage, and to disperse the families I have an aversion. What then is to be done? Something must, or I shall be ruined. . . .[10]

Washington knew that many freed slaves would have no way of earning a living. He was unwilling to free some workers while keeping others enslaved.[11] To make matters more complicated, every slave state had laws against simply letting slaves go. The legal process to free them was difficult and expensive.[12]

Washington tried breaking up his property into smaller farms and renting out these farms without slaves. He hoped that his tenants would agree to hire freed slaves on the same terms as any other workers.[13] Unfortunately, Washington found that he could not rent out the farms without including slaves.

Before his death, he decided on the best solution he could think of.

A Dream, a Decision, and Death

In the summer of 1799, Washington dreamed about an angel and interpreted it as a warning of his own death.[14] He started working on his will.

Washington wrote in his will careful instructions that his slaves would be freed upon his wife's death. Those who could not work would be given a pension. In addition, the children of freed slaves would be supported until they were old enough to earn a living. They would be taught to read and write, as well as useful occupations.[15]

On December 12, 1799, when he was sixty-eight, Washington rode about his farms on horseback just as usual. The morning was cold. By afternoon, it was snowing and windy. Wet and cold, Washington returned from his ride with snow in his hair. The next morning, he had a sore throat, but he still went out to mark some trees that were to be cut down. By evening, his voice was very hoarse. The next day, Washington had chills and could barely speak.

The family called in doctors, who tried various remedies, including a mixture of molasses, vinegar, and butter, and a gargle of vinegar and sage tea.

They also bled the patient. But nothing helped. Washington could barely breathe.

George Washington died on the evening of December 14, 1799. The nation went into deep mourning.[16]

After Washington's death, Martha Washington was left with more than three hundred slaves at Mount Vernon. About half of them had been owned by George Washington. The rest were her own. According to Washington's will, his slaves were to be free after his death. He also laid out

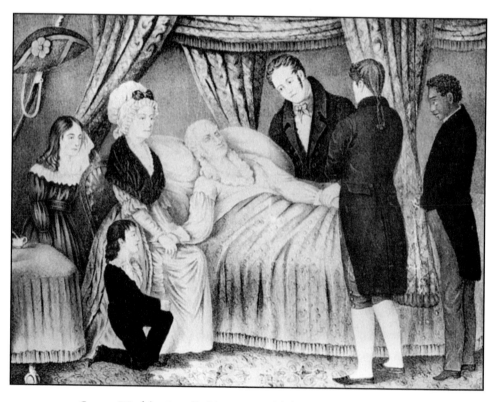

George Washington died in 1799 with his wife, Martha, at his side.

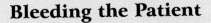

Bleeding the Patient

With their limited understanding of medicine, physicians of George Washington's time often did their patients more harm than good. When a patient was seriously ill, doctors often assumed that it was because of impure blood—or even too much blood. So, doctors would cut a vein or artery and let some of the patient's blood flow out. Because of this practice, many patients actually became weaker under their doctors' care. Washington's physicians bled him several times, removing about five pints of blood in all, hastening his death.

instructions in his will for the continued care and education of some of his former slaves, provided support and training for young people until they came of age and took care of old people.

Until 1833, Washington's heirs paid pensions to the freed slaves who could not work. However, the heirs could not carry out Washington's plans to educate the children because Virginia passed laws against educating African Americans.[17]

Remembering Washington

SOON AFTER GEORGE Washington died, a speech made in the United States Senate in December 1779 urged Americans to "teach their children never to forget that the fruit of his labors and his example are their inheritance."[1] Today, people are familiar with the fruits of Washington's labors. Working with others, he helped create the United States. But the word "example" is also very important when one thinks about George Washington. In a Public Broadcasting Services (PBS) television series, *Rediscovering George Washington*, historian Richard Brookhiser compared George Washington to Babe Ruth and Mark McGwire. People with such great gifts and accomplishments, Brookhiser added, show the rest of us what is possible. They make human potential visible.[2]

Washington knew people—such as Alexander Hamilton and Thomas Jefferson—who spent a lot of time discussing exciting ideas. Washington also talked about ideas, but he was most truly a man of action.[3] To Washington, an important idea was much more than words. It was a standard to live up to. He became a hero because of the kind of man he was and because of the things he did, more than for anything he said.

Creating a Country

A 1778 almanac may have been the first to call George Washington the "Father of His country."[4]

Words and Deeds

Many of Washington's fellow founders expressed themselves in thrilling language. The very voice of Thomas Jefferson comes alive to us in stirring phrases like, "We hold these truths to be self-evident, that all men are created equal. . . ." Washington seldom used words like that, but he carefully considered the pros and cons of every issue before making a speech, writing a letter, or issuing a proclamation. With his deeds and actions, Washington gave meaning to the often more eloquent words of others.

George Washington

(An almanac is a yearly publication that usually includes a calendar, information, sayings, and stories.) By the time he became president, the title had become popular, and Washington has been called that ever since. Washington and other leaders of the American Revolution are often called the founding fathers. But some historians believe that without George Washington, there might not have been a United States of America. Or if there was, America would be very different from how the country is today.

For example, without Washington, America might have lost the Revolutionary War. No other military leader won the admiration of the fighting men like Washington did. The army followed Washington through battles against larger, better-trained forces. Men stayed with him during freezing weather and in terrible living conditions. Washington also knew how to deal with members of the Continental Congress upon whom the army depended for supplies and weapons. It is likely that, under any other commander, the Continental army would have fallen apart.

Even if the army had managed to win the war without Washington, the new country might not have remained together. The delegates to the Constitutional Convention knew that America needed a strong central government to keep the new states united. The government they worked out—with executive, legislative, and judicial branches—has held the United States together for

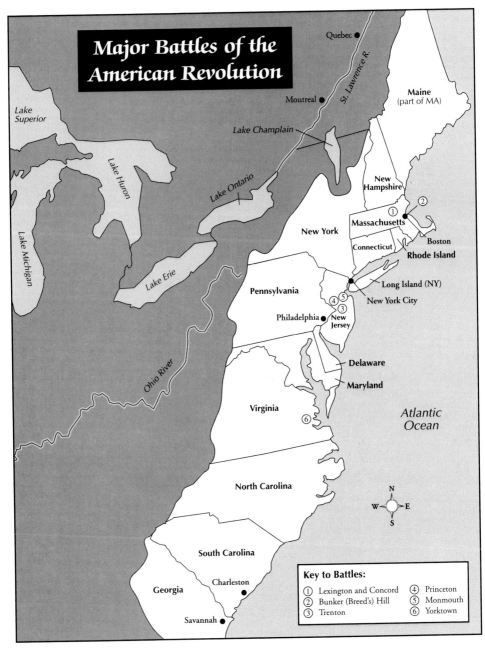

Major Battles of the American Revolution

Quebec ●

Montreal ●

St. Lawrence R.

Maine (part of MA)

Lake Superior

Lake Champlain

Lake Huron

Lake Ontario

New Hampshire

Lake Michigan

Lake Erie

New York

① ②

Massachusetts

Boston

Connecticut

Rhode Island

Pennsylvania

Long Island (NY)

④ ⑤ ③

New York City

Philadelphia ●

New Jersey

Ohio River

Delaware

Maryland

Virginia

⑥

Atlantic Ocean

N
W E
S

North Carolina

South Carolina

Key to Battles:

① Lexington and Concord ④ Princeton
② Bunker (Breed's) Hill   ⑤ Monmouth
③ Trenton   ⑥ Yorktown

Georgia

Charleston ●

Savannah ●

This map shows some of the major battles of the American Revolution. These battles were fought under Washington's brave leadership.

more than two hundred years. But some delegates only agreed to include the executive position because they knew that a completely trustworthy person—Washington—was available to be president.[5]

The delegates to the Constitutional Convention admired Washington because he had demonstrated his ability to lead. More importantly, they trusted Washington because he had shown his willingness to give up power.

For some people, the lure of power is too strong to resist. Throughout history, successful revolutions have often led to tyranny. The military that wins a war often refuses to give up power. Politicians who think they cannot get the country organized any other way often resort to force. George Washington was able to stand firm against any temptation to take all the power for himself.

At the end of the Revolutionary War, Washington gave up his military position and retired. He agreed to become president only when others convinced him that the country desperately needed him. After two terms in office, he stepped aside again so that power could be peacefully transferred to another president.

Our country's founders were absolutely right when they decided to trust George Washington. He was completely committed to civilian rule of the United States. He also believed that educated men of good will could work together. He respected those around him and was willing to compromise with them. He constantly urged others to put aside their differences of opinion and to work together on whatever was best for the country.

How We Remember Washington

Washington became a legend, even during his lifetime. In battle, his personal bravery and fearlessness under fire both startled and inspired his men.[6] When the government was being formed, the slightest sign of Washington's opinion could often carry an argument.

After his death, stories about Washington became even more exaggerated. In the early 1800s, a minister named Mason Weems believed that a man like Washington must have been noble even in childhood. Because no appropriate stories seemed to be available, Weems made some up. He published them in a book about Washington.

Weems's story about "George Washington and the Cherry Tree" was retold—often in simpler versions—in many books for children.[7] For many people, the fictional line "I cannot tell a lie" became George Washington's most famous saying.[8] But the real Washington did many braver and more difficult things than those in Weems's stories.

Today, we often think of Washington as being stiff and formal. That is partly because most portraits painted during his time made everybody look stiff and formal. Besides, when George Washington was older, his artificial teeth were uncomfortable

When George . . . was about six years old, he was made the wealthy master of a <u>hatchet</u>! . . . and was constantly going about chopping every thing that came in his way. One day, in the garden . . . he unluckily tried the edge of his hatchet on the body of a beautiful young English cherry-tree, which he barked so terribly, that I don't believe the tree ever got the better of it. The next morning the old gentleman finding out what had befallen his tree . . . came into the house, and with much warmth asked for the mischievous author. . . . Presently George and his hatchet made their appearance. <u>George, said his father, do you know who killed that beautiful little cherry-tree yonder in the garden?</u> This was a <u>tough question</u>: and George staggered under it for a moment; but quickly recovered himself: and looking at his father . . . he bravely cried out, <u>"I can't tell a lie, Pa; you know I can't tell a lie. I did cut it with my hatchet."—Run to my arms, you dearest boy,</u> cried his father in transports, <u>run to my arms; glad am I, George, that you killed my tree; for you have paid me for it a thousand fold. Such an act of heroism in my son, is more worth than a thousand trees, though blossomed with silver, and their fruits of purest gold.</u>[9]

In 1809, a minister named Mason Weems published a book about George Washington. Weems made up many of the stories, such as this one about young Washington and a cherry tree.

and made it difficult to smile. It is true that Washington's dignified presence created quite an impression on those around him. Early in life, he had decided that being formal was often the best way to get things done. But he was also a man of great energy and enthusiasm.

George Washington was the teenager who struggled through the wilderness, spending time with American Indians and frontiersmen. He was the young officer who amazed other soldiers with his athletic ability and courage. Washington was also the Revolutionary War commander who leaped up and down in joy—and astonished a French general with a hug—when he heard that help was on the way from France.

As a military leader, Washington charged into battle ahead of his men, shouting "It's a fine fox chase, my boys," as he pursued fleeing British troops.[10]

Mason Weems published a book about George Washington that featured famous legends about the first president of the United States.

He was the aging warrior who won over his angry officers at Newburgh by showing them his frailty and humanity. And as the president of the Constitutional Convention, Washington often advised delegates with nothing more than a smile or a scowl.

His mind was great and powerful, without being of the very first order.... He was incapable of fear, meeting personal dangers with the calmest unconcern. Perhaps the strongest feature in his character was prudence, never acting until every circumstance, every consideration, was maturely weighed; refraining if he saw a doubt, but, when once decided, going through with his purpose, whatever obstacles opposed. His integrity was most pure, his justice the most inflexible I have ever known.... He was, indeed, in every sense of the words, a wise, a good, and a great man. His temper was naturally high toned; but reflection and resolution had obtained a firm and habitual ascendancy over it. If ever, however, it broke its bonds, he was most tremendous in his wrath.... His heart was not warm in its affections; but he exactly calculated every man's value, and gave him a solid esteem proportioned to it. His person, you know, was fine, his stature exactly what one would wish, his deportment easy, erect and noble; the best horseman of his age, and the most graceful figure that could be seen on horseback....

On the whole, his character was, in its mass, perfect, in nothing bad, in few points indifferent; and it may truly be said, that never did nature and fortune combine more perfectly to make a man great....[11]

These lines are from a letter that Thomas Jefferson wrote about George Washington fourteen years after Washington's death.

All his life, George Washington struggled to be what he thought a good man should be. Fortunately, that included commitment, a spirit of adventure, boundless strength and energy, a self-critical nature, and willingness to compromise with others.

Timeline

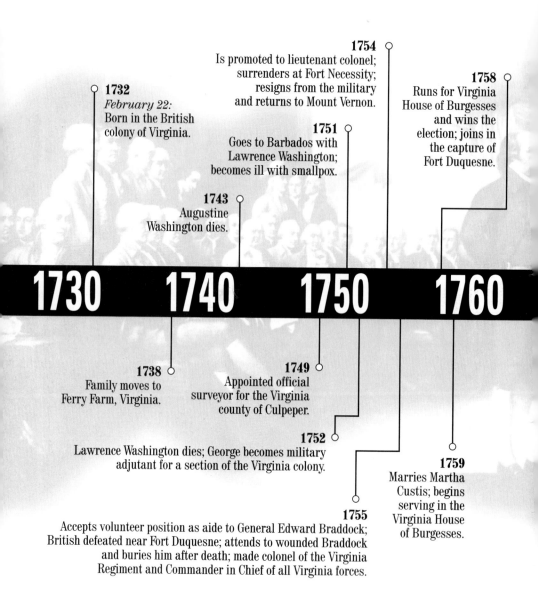

1754
Is promoted to lieutenant colonel; surrenders at Fort Necessity; resigns from the military and returns to Mount Vernon.

1758
Runs for Virginia House of Burgesses and wins the election; joins in the capture of Fort Duquesne.

1732
February 22:
Born in the British colony of Virginia.

1751
Goes to Barbados with Lawrence Washington; becomes ill with smallpox.

1743
Augustine Washington dies.

1730 1740 1750 1760

1738
Family moves to Ferry Farm, Virginia.

1749
Appointed official surveyor for the Virginia county of Culpeper.

Lawrence Washington dies; George becomes military adjutant for a section of the Virginia colony.

1752

1759
Marries Martha Custis; begins serving in the Virginia House of Burgesses.

1755
Accepts volunteer position as aide to General Edward Braddock; British defeated near Fort Duquesne; attends to wounded Braddock and buries him after death; made colonel of the Virginia Regiment and Commander in Chief of all Virginia forces.

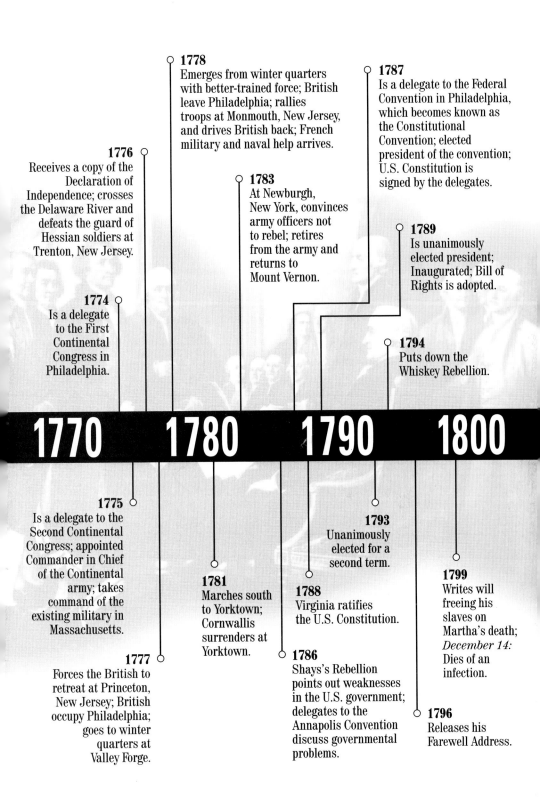

1776
Receives a copy of the Declaration of Independence; crosses the Delaware River and defeats the guard of Hessian soldiers at Trenton, New Jersey.

1774
Is a delegate to the First Continental Congress in Philadelphia.

1778
Emerges from winter quarters with better-trained force; British leave Philadelphia; rallies troops at Monmouth, New Jersey, and drives British back; French military and naval help arrives.

1783
At Newburgh, New York, convinces army officers not to rebel; retires from the army and returns to Mount Vernon.

1787
Is a delegate to the Federal Convention in Philadelphia, which becomes known as the Constitutional Convention; elected president of the convention; U.S. Constitution is signed by the delegates.

1789
Is unanimously elected president; Inaugurated; Bill of Rights is adopted.

1794
Puts down the Whiskey Rebellion.

1770　1780　1790　1800

1775
Is a delegate to the Second Continental Congress; appointed Commander in Chief of the Continental army; takes command of the existing military in Massachusetts.

1777
Forces the British to retreat at Princeton, New Jersey; British occupy Philadelphia; goes to winter quarters at Valley Forge.

1781
Marches south to Yorktown; Cornwallis surrenders at Yorktown.

1786
Shays's Rebellion points out weaknesses in the U.S. government; delegates to the Annapolis Convention discuss governmental problems.

1788
Virginia ratifies the U.S. Constitution.

1793
Unanimously elected for a second term.

1799
Writes will freeing his slaves on Martha's death; *December 14:* Dies of an infection.

1796
Releases his Farewell Address.

Chapter Notes

Chapter 1. Conspiracy

1. George Washington, "Letter to John Armstrong, January 10, 1783," *George Washington Papers at the Library of Congress*, n.d., <http://memory.loc.gov/ammem/gwhtml/gwhome.html> (June 14, 2003).

2. James Thomas Flexner, *Washington: The Indispensable Man* (New York: Little, Brown and Company, 1974), p. 172.

3. Douglas Southall Freeman, *Washington*, ed. Richard Harwell (New York: Charles Scribner's Sons, 1968), p. 500.

4. Ibid.

5. Ibid.

6. John Ferling, *Setting the World Ablaze: Washington, Adams, Jefferson, and the American Revolution* (New York: Oxford University Press, 2000), p. 266.

7. Ibid., p. 267.

8. George Washington, "Speech to the Officers of the Army, Head Quarters, Newburgh, March 15, 1783," *Public Broadcasting Services*, n.d., <http://www.pbs.org/georgewashington/milestones/newburgh_read.html> (June 15, 2003).

9. Freeman, p. 501.

10. Ferling, p. 268.

11. Ibid.

12. George L. Marshall, Jr., "The Rise and Fall of the Newburgh Conspiracy: How General Washington and his Spectacles Saved the Republic," n.d., <http://earlyamerica.com/review/fall97/wshngton.html> (June 15, 2003).

13. Worthington C. Ford, ed., *Journals of the Continental Congress, 1774–1789*, 1904–1937, <memory.loc.gov/ammem/amlaw/lawhome.html> (June 15, 2003).

Chapter 2. From Country Boy to Virginia Gentleman

1. Douglas Southall Freeman, *Washington*, ed. Richard Harwell (New York: Charles Scribner's Sons, 1968), p. 6.

2. "Frequently Asked Questions, George Washington 1732–1799," n.d., <http://gwpapers.virginia.edu/faq/index.html> (June 15, 2003).

3. Ibid., pp. 1–2.

4. Ibid., p. 3.

5. John Ferling, *Setting the World Ablaze: Washington, Adams, Jefferson, and the American Revolution* (New York: Oxford University Press, 2000), p. 14.

6. Richard Brookhiser, *Founding Father: Rediscovering George Washington* (New York: Free Press, 1996), p. 162.

7. Freeman, p. 8.

8. Brookhiser, p. 163.

9. "Washington's School Exercises: Rules of Civility & Decent Behaviour In Company and Conversation," *The Papers of George Washington, University of Virginia,* n.d., <http://gwpapers.virginia.edu/civility/index.html> (June 15, 2003).

10. Freeman, p. 10.

11. Brookhiser, p. 111.

12. Ferling, p. 14.

13. Ibid., p. 15.

14. Freeman, p. 17.

15. George Washington "A survey of the northern neck of Virginia, 1747," *The Diaries of George Washington, George Washington Papers at the Library of Congress,* 1976, <http://memory.loc.gov/ammem/gwhtml/gwhome.html> (June 14, 2003).

16. Freeman, p. 18.

17. George Washington "A Journal of my Journey over the Mountains began Fryday the 11th. of March 1747/8," *The Diaries of George Washington, George Washington Papers at the Library of Congress,* 1976, <http://memory.loc.gov/ammem/gwhtml/gwhome.html> (June 14, 2003).

18. Ibid., p. 12.

19. Freeman, p. 20.

20. Washington, "A Journal of my Journey over the Mountains began Fryday the 11th. of March 1747/8," p. 13.

21. Freeman, p. 21.

22. Washington, "A Journal of my Journey over the Mountains began Fryday the 11th. of March 1747/8," p. 13.

23. The Colonial Music Institute, "Bringing History to Life Through Music: An Iroquois Dance," n.d., <http://www.colonialmusic.org/Resource/Indians.htm> (June 15, 2003).

24. Ibid.

25. "A Journal of my Journey over the Mountains began Fryday the 11th. of March 1747/8," p. 13.

Chapter 3. Growing Up Fast

1. Douglas Southall Freeman, *Washington*, ed. Richard Harwell (New York: Charles Scribner's Sons, 1968), p. 24.

2. John Ferling, *Setting the World Ablaze: Washington, Adams, Jefferson, and the American Revolution* (New York: Oxford University Press, 2000), p. 15.

3. Ibid.

4. Ibid.

5. Freeman, pp. 28–30.

6. Ibid., p. 29.

7. Richard Brookhiser, *Founding Father: Rediscovering George Washington* (New York: Free Press, 1996), p. 153.

8. James Thomas Flexner, *Washington: The Indispensable Man* (New York: Little, Brown and Company, 1974), p. 8.

9. Ibid.

10. Ibid., p. 7.

11. Freeman, pp. 32–33.

12. Ibid., p. 33.

Chapter 4. The Young Officer

1. John Ferling, *Setting the World Ablaze: Washington, Adams, Jefferson, and the American Revolution* (New York: Oxford University Press, 2000), p. 16.

2. Ibid.

3. James Thomas Flexner, *Washington: The Indispensable Man* (New York: Little, Brown and Company, 1974), p. 11.

4. Garry Wills, *Cincinnatus: George Washington and the Enlightenment* (New York: Doubleday, 1984), p. 128.

5. Forrest McDonald, "Presidential Character: The Example of George Washington," *Perspectives on Political Science*, June 22, 1997.

6. Flexner, pp. 11–15.

7. Ibid., p. 13.

8. Ibid.

9. Ibid.

10. Douglas Southall Freeman, *Washington*, ed. Richard Harwell (New York: Charles Scribner's Sons, 1968), p. 45.

11. Ibid.

12. Ibid.

13. Ibid., p. 46.

14. George Washington "Letter to his brother, John Augustine," *The Diaries of George Washington, George Washington Papers at the Library of Congress*, 1976, <http://memory.loc.gov/ammem/gwhtml/gwhome.html> (June 14, 2003).

15. Freeman, p. 84

16. George Washington, "Letter to Mary Ball Washington, July 18, 1755," *George Washington Papers at the Library of Congress*, <http://memory.loc.gov/ammem/gwhtml/gwhome.html> (June 14, 2003).

17. Freeman, p. 91.

18. Flexner, p. 28.

19. Ferling, p. 32.

20. Freeman, p. 123.

Chapter 5. A Man of Power

1. John Ferling, *Setting the World Ablaze: Washington, Adams, Jefferson, and the American Revolution* (New York: Oxford University Press, 2000), p. 33.

2. James Thomas Flexner, *Washington: The Indispensable Man* (New York: Little, Brown and Company, 1974), p. 39.

3. Ibid.

4. Ibid., p. 48.

5. Richard Brookhiser, *Founding Father: Rediscovering George Washington* (New York: Free Press, 1996), p. 153.

6. Ibid., p. 139.

7. Flexner, p. 52.

8. Ibid., p. 54.

9. Douglas Southall Freeman, *Washington*, ed. Richard Harwell (New York: Charles Scribner's Sons, 1968), p. 150.

10. Flexner, pp. 47–49.

11. Ibid., p. 49.

12. Ibid., p. 58.

13. Ibid.

14. Ibid., p. 59.

15. Ferling, p. 107.

Chapter 6. The General and the American Revolution

1. John Ferling, *Setting the World Ablaze: Washington, Adams, Jefferson, and the American Revolution* (New York: Oxford University Press, 2000), p. 33.

2. Ibid.

3. James Thomas Flexner, *Washington: The Indispensable Man* (New York: Little, Brown and Company, 1974), p. 68.

4. Ibid., p. 69.

5. Ferling, p. 115

6. Ibid., p. 120.

7. Ibid., p. 119.

8. Flexner, p. 79.

9. Richard Brookhiser, *Founding Father: Rediscovering George Washington* (New York: Free Press, 1996), p. 17.

10. Flexner, pp. 83–84.

11. Ferling, p. 145.

12. Ibid.

13. Flexner, p. 94.

14. Ferling, p. 146.

15. Flexner, p. 95.

16. Ibid.

17. Brookhiser, p. 29.

18. Flexner, pp. 95–96.

19. "George Washington and the Society of the Cincinnati," *The Papers of George Washington, University of Virginia,* n.d., <http://gwpapers.virginia.edu/articles/cincinnati/> (June 15, 2003).

20. Ferling, pp. 186–187.

21. Flexner, p. 117.

22. Ibid., p. 118.

23. Albigence Waldo "From the Diary of Albigence Waldo, Surgeon at Valley Forge, 1777," *From Revolution to Reconstruction,* April 18, 2003, <http://odur.let.rug.nl/~usa/D/1776-1800/war/waldo.htm> (June 16, 2003).

24. Ibid., p. 119.

25. Brookhiser, p. 32.

26. "Milestones: Battle of Monmouth 1778," *Public Broadcasting Service,* n.d., <http://www.pbs.org/georgewashington/milestones/monmouth_about.html> (June 16, 2003).

27. Ibid.

28. Brookhiser, p. 33.

29. Freeman, p. 471.

30. Ibid., p. 472.

31. Flexner, p. 160.

32. George Washington "Washington's Farewell Address to the Army, Rocky Hill, New Jersey, 2 November 1783," *The Papers of George Washington, University of Virginia,* n.d., <http://gwpapers.virginia.edu/revolution/farewell/index.html> (June 15, 2003).

Chapter 7. From Confusion to a Constitution

1. "Frequently Asked Questions," *The Papers of George Washington, University of Virginia,* n.d., <http://gwpapers.virginia. edu/faq/govern.html> (June 15, 2003).

2. James Thomas Flexner, *Washington: The Indispensable Man* (New York: Little, Brown and Company, 1974), p. 183.

3. John Hunter "Mr. John Hunter, an English visitor to Mt. Vernon in 1785, in a letter to a friend," n.d., *Valley Forge FAQS, Historic Valley Forge* <http://www.ushistory.org/valleyforge/youasked/024.htm> (June 15, 2003).

4. Richard Brookhiser, *Founding Father: Rediscovering George Washington* (New York: Free Press, 1996), p. 48.

5. Flexner, p. 223.

6. Ibid., p. 190.

7. Ibid., p. 200.

8. Ibid., p. 207.

9. William Steele "William Steele to Jonathan D. Steele," *The Records of the Federal Convention of 1787, The Library of Congress,* n.d., <http://memory.loc.gov> (June 16, 2003).

10. The Constitution of the United States of America.

11. Benjamin Franklin, "Address to the Federal Convention, 1787," *U.S. Constitution Americans.net*, n.d., <http://www.usconstitution.com/BenjaminFranklinat ConstitutionalConvention.htm> (June 16, 2003).

12. George Washington, "Letters to Patrick Henry, Benjamin Harrison, and Thomas Nelson Jr., September 24, 1787," *George Washington Papers at the Library of Congress*, n.d., <http://memory.loc.gov/ammem/gwhtml/gwhome.html> (June 14, 2003).

13. James Monroe, "Letter to Thomas Jefferson, July 12, 1788," *George Washington Papers at the Library of Congress*, n.d., <http://memory.loc.gov/ammem/gwhtml/gwhome.html> (June 14, 2003).

Chapter 8. The First President

1. Richard Brookhiser, *Founding Father: Rediscovering George Washington* (New York: Free Press, 1996), p. 41.

2. George Washington "Letters to Mary Cranch, 9 Aug. 1789, 5 Jan. and 27 July 1790," *The Diaries of George Washington, George Washington Papers at the Library of Congress,* 1979, <http://memory.loc.gov/ammem/gwhtml/gwhome .html> (June 14, 2003).

3. Forrest McDonald, "Presidential Character: The Example of George Washington," *Perspectives on Political Science*, June 22, 1997.

4. Stuart Leibiger, "Founding Friendship: Washington, Madison and the Creation of the American Republic," *History Today*, July 1, 2001, p. 21.

5. U.S. Senate: Historical Minute Essays, "April 27,1789, The Senate Prepares for a President," n. d., <http://senate/gov/artandhistory/history/minute/The_Senate_Prepares_For_A_President.htm> (June 16, 2003).

6. Leibiger, p. 21.

7. George Washington, "Letter to Catherine Macaulay Graham, January 9, 1790," *George Washington Papers at the Library of Congress*, <http://memory.loc.gov/ammem/gwhtml/gwhome.html> (June 14, 2003).

8. George Roche, "George Washington's Legacy," *USA Today Magazine*, vol. 127, May 1, 1999.

9. "George Washington and the Rule of Law: 3. Washington and the Whiskey Rebellion," *Public Broadcasting Service*, n.d., <http://www.pbs.org/georgewashington/classroom/rule_of_law.html> (June 16, 2003).

10. James Thomas Flexner, *Washington: The Indispensable Man* (New York: Little, Brown and Company, 1974), p. 300.

Chapter 9. A Hero's Final Years

1. James Thomas Flexner, *Washington: The Indispensable Man* (New York: Little, Brown and Company, 1974), p. 360.

2. George Washington, "Letter to James McHenry, May 29, 1797," *George Washington Papers at the Library of Congress*, n.d., <http://memory.loc.gov/ammem/gwhtml/gwhome.html> (June 14, 2003).

3. Ibid.

4. Flexner, p. 365.

5. Ibid., p. 368.

6. George Washington "George Washington to James McHenry," *The Writings of George Washington from the Original Manuscript Sources, 1745–1799*, May 29, 1797, <http://memory.loc.gov/ammem/gwhtml/gwhome.html> (June 14, 2003).

7. Flexner, pp. 386–388.

8. Ibid., p. 385.

9. W. W. Abbot, "George Washington in Retirement," *The Papers of George Washington*, December 5, 1999, <http://gwpapers.virginia.edu/articles/retire/index.html> (June 15, 2003).

10. Ibid.

11. Ibid.

12. "George Washington and the Problem of Slavery," n.d., *Public Broadcasting Service,* <http://www.pbs.org/georgewashington/classroom/slavery2.html> (June 16, 2003).

13. Flexner, p. 388.

14. John Ferling, *Setting the World Ablaze: Washington, Adams, Jefferson, and the American Revolution* (New York: Oxford University Press, 2000), p. 296.

15. Flexner, p. 393.

16. Mary Anne Andrei, "Introduction," in *A Concert of Mourning*, 1999, <http://www.gwpapers.virginia.edu/exhibits/mourning/front.html> (June 15, 2003).

17. George Washington "From George Washington's Last Will," *Papers of George Washington, University of Virginia,* n.d., <http://www.gwpapers.virginia.edu/slavery> (June 15, 2003).

Chapter 10. Remembering Washington

1. "Address to the President of the United States, on the death of General George Washington, Monday, December 23, 1799," *Journal of the Senate of the United States of America, 1789–1873, George Washington Papers at the Library of Congress,* n.d., <http://memory.loc.gov/ammem/gwhtml/gwhome.html> (June 14, 2003).

2. "Washington: Father of His Country," *Public Broadcasting Service,* n.d., <http://www.pbs.org/georgewashington/father/index.html> (June 16, 2003).

3. Garry Wills, *Cincinnatus: George Washington and the Enlightenment* (New York: Doubleday, 1984), p. 130.

4. Richard Brookhiser, *Founding Father: Rediscovering George Washington* (New York: Free Press, 1996), p. 159.

5. Forrest McDonald, "Presidential Character: the Example of George Washington," *Perspectives on Political Science*, June 22, 1997.

6. "George Washington: The Commander in Chief," <http://www.ushistory.org/valleyforge/washington/george2html> (June 11, 2003).

7. Wills, p. 52.

8. Brookhiser, p. 192.

9. Mason L. Weems "The Fable of George Washington and the Cherry Tree," *Papers of George Washington, University of Virginia,* n.d., <http://gwpapers.virginia.edu/documents/weems/index. html> (June 5, 2003).

10. "George Washington as Military Leader: 3. Washington's Important Revolutionary War Victories," *Public Broadcasting Service,* n.d., <http://www.pbs.org/georgewashington/classroom/military_leader2.html> (June 15, 2003).

11. Thomas Jefferson "Thomas Jefferson on George Washington," *Public Broadcasting Service,* n.d., <http://www.pbs.org/georgewashington/multimedia/sajak/thomas_jefferson.html> (June 15, 2003).

Glossary

anonymous—The author's name is not known or given.

British—Relating to the people or property of the United Kingdom of Great Britain.

commission—An appointment to a particular position or rank.

Confederation—The union of the original thirteen states under the Articles of Confederation.

conspiracy—A plot to commit an illegal or insubordinate action.

delegate—A representative who acts on behalf of an organization or government.

dictatorship—A government ruled by a leader with absolute power.

diplomat—One who represents his or her government in another country.

English—The people or language of England.

enlist—To enroll in the military.

executive—Relating to the part of government that ensures laws are carried out.

fortification—Structure built to strengthen defenses, such as a wall or ditch.

judicial—Relating to the branch of government that decides legal issues and administers justice in the courts.

legislative—Relating to the branch of government that writes laws.

legislature—The part of government with the power to make and change laws.

profession—An occupation that requires a great deal of education and training.

regiment—A permanent military unit under the command of a colonel, and consisting of smaller units, such as companies.

republic—A nation that is governed by representatives who are chosen by the citizens.

tactics—Plans for moving forces during warfare.

tenant—Someone who rents property for a specific period of time.

Further Reading

Books

Collier, Christopher, and James Lincoln Collier. *Creating the Constitution: 1787.* Tarrytown, N.Y.: Marshall Cavendish Corporation, 1999.

Collins, Mary. *Mount Vernon.* Danbury, Conn.: Children's Press, 1998.

Ferrie, Richard. *The World Turned Upside Down: George Washington and the Battle of Yorktown.* New York: Holiday House, Inc., 1998.

Fradin, Dennis Brindell. *The Signers: The Fifty-six Stories Behind the Declaration of Independence.* New York: Walker, 2002.

Leebrick, Kristal. *The Constitution.* Mankato, Minn.: Capstone Press, Inc., 2002.

McClung, Robert M. *Young George Washington and the French and Indian War, 1753–1758.* North Haven, Conn.: Shoe String Press, 2002.

Morris, Jeffrey. *The Washington Way.* Minneapolis, Minn.: Lerner Publications, 1994.

Rosenberg, John M. *First in Peace: George Washington, the Constitution and the Presidency.* Brookfield, Conn.: Millbrook Press, Inc., 1998.

Weidner, Ed.D., Daniel. *The Constitution.* Berkeley Heights, N.J.: Enslow Publishers, Inc., 2002.

Internet Addresses

Independence Hall Association. "The Unsolved Mystery of Graves and Ghosts at Valley Forge." *Historic Valley Forge*. ©1998–2003. <http://www.ushistory.org/valleyforge/history/vmyster.html>.

National Museum of American History, Smithsonian Institute. "George Washington 1732–1799." *The American Presidency: A Glorious Burden*. © 2003. <http://www.americanhistory.si.edu/presidency/timeline/timeline.html>.

Whitten, Chris. "FoundingFathers.info." ©2001–2003. <http://www.foundingfathers.info/>.

Places to Visit

Colonial National Historical Park
P.O. Box 210
Yorktown, Virginia 23690
(757) 229-1733
<http://www.nps.gov/colo/>

Federal Hall National Memorial
26 Wall Street
New York, New York 10005
(212) 825-6888
<http://www.nps.gov/feha/>

Fort Necessity National Battlefield
1 Washington Parkway
Farmington, Pennsylvania 15437
(724) 329-5805
<http://www.nps.gov/fone/index.htm>

George Washington Birthplace National Monument
1732 Popes Creek Road
Washington's Birthplace, Virginia 22443-5115
(804) 224-1732
<http://www.nps.gov/gewa>

Valley Forge National Historic Park
P.O. Box 953
Valley Forge, Pennsylvania 19482-0953
(610) 783-1077
<http://nps.gov/vafo/>

Washington Monument
900 Ohio Drive, SW
Washington, D.C. 20024-2000
(202) 426-6841
<http://www.nps.gov/wamo/>

Index